No. 47 Squadron, RFC in Macedonia and Russia, 1916-19

No. 47 Squadron, RFC in Macedonia and Russia, 1916-19

A First Hand Account and History by a Serving Officer

ILLUSTRATED

Over the Balkans and South Russia

and

Macedonia–Final Air Operations,1918

H. A. Jones

with

A Bombing Stunt and Afterwards

by Ballast

LEONAUR

No. 47 Squadron, RAF in Macedonia and Russia, 1916-19
A First Hand Account and History by a Serving Officer
Over the Balkans and South Russia
and
Macedonia-Final Air Operations, 1918
by H. A. Jones
with
A Bombing Stunt and Afterwards
by Ballast

ILLUSTRATED

FIRST EDITION IN THIS FORM

First published in the titles
Over the Balkans and South Russia
War in the Air 6 (Extract)
and
Blackwood's Magazine 1918-10 Vol. 204 Iss. 1236 (Extract)

Leonaur is an imprint of Oakpast Ltd
Copyright in this form © 2025 Oakpast Ltd

ISBN: 978-1-917666-12-1 (hardcover)
ISBN: 978-1-917666-13-8 (softcover)

http://www.leonaur.com

Publisher's Notes

Contents

Preface

An army may march on its stomach, a squadron flies on its spirit. The pilots and observers if they are not light-hearted, will, in the words of Sir Walter Raleigh, do worse than die.

The air service is new and its traditions are recent. Many of those who served in a squadron during the war knew little of its past history, or heard only vaguely of what happened when they were no longer with the unit. Those squadrons which are now on the permanent list of the Royal Air Force were chosen because of their record in the war. Unless the record is written, there is danger of the tradition being lost.

This brief history of the work in the war of one of the permanent squadrons is based chiefly on the records of No. 47 Squadron and of the 16th Wing, in possession of the Air Historical Branch. For the interpretation of those records, the author alone is responsible. Some of the squadron documents are missing, but past members and friends of the squadron have come forward with personal diaries to fill up the gaps.

Many of those who did splendid work with No. 47 find no mention in these pages. They spent their time on the routine work of a corps squadron: spotting for the artillery; taking photographs; on reconnaissance over the difficult mountains of Macedonia or the mud-flooded plains of South Russia. Any attempt to catalogue their reports would make tedious reading. They will, I hope, be content with this effort to tell what that work was, and to let their tribute pass on to those whose life's work ended with the squadron.

To my late colleague, J. C. Nerney, I give grateful thanks for the maps. To D. F. Woodford, the original adjutant, who contributed so much towards the efficiency of 47, I am indebted. His patient zeal has done not a little to bring this history into production. L. P. Sedgwick, who served long with the squadron, has kindly supplied the blocks for the maps and photographs. To all those others whose generosity has helped to make the publication of the book possible, I am deeply grateful.

H. A. Jones.

Foreword

By Air Vice-Marshal Sir W. G. H. Salmond, K.C.M.G., C.B., D.S.O.

The Royal Air Force, Middle East, embraced an operational air area which no command in any service has hitherto approached. With its headquarters in Egypt, where its principal depots were established, it administered and directed the methods of operation of squadrons operating with the different Army Commands in Salonika, Palestine, Mesopotamia, East Africa, the Western Desert of Egypt, and the Soudan. The duties of its pilots were varied in the extreme.

No. 47 Squadron may be quoted as a typical example of a Middle East squadron. Not only did it operate on the Salonika front, but it took part in the air operations with the French on the Monastir front, and later it transferred its activities to the Russian front, where, with General Denikin, by its concentrated air offensive it more than once turned the scale decisively in favour of the anti-Bolshevist Forces. Nor were its activities confined to operations against land forces, but in January, 1918, it attacked the *Goeben* after her sortie from the Dardanelles, when she ran aground off Nagara Point.

Little did we think, when war was declared on August 4th, 1914, how diverse would be the duties which our youth would be called upon to carry out for England's sake. Little did these young pilots think, when they were training in England in 1914 and 1915, that that training would be subsequently translated into combats with German machines over the mountains of Macedonia, or that they would be starting off in the cold dusk of an early morning laden with bombs, protected by their brother-pilots in fighting scouts, with a mission to destroy hostile aircraft located in some mountain aerodrome in Bulgaria.

Nor did they think that, day in and day out, they would be watching the German-Bulgarian lines in the Salonika Command and directing the fire of our guns against Bulgarian objectives, or that they would be starting off on a 200-mile flight from their home aerodrome to attack a great German battleship run aground in the Dardanelles, or that they later would carry out a decisive air offensive against the whole Bulgarian Army retreating through the defiles from the Salonika front to the plains of Bulgaria.

Nor probably did they envisage the tremendous results that such an air offensive and their active part in it could have on the fortunes of the Great War, for the repeated air attacks of the Salonika Air Force on the retreating Bulgarian Army smashed the transport to atoms and compelled the Bulgarians to abandon their artillery and all their means of resuming the fight, with the result that they sued for peace. Nor did these same young pilots imagine that they would be called upon to represent their country with the Russian Army struggling in South Russia in the spring of 1919.

In all these operations officers and men of No. 47 Squadron carried out their duties with splendid efficiency, and displayed a bravery, tenacity, and adaptability to all circumstances in keeping with the highest traditions of our Fighting Forces.

The story of these things is told in the following pages. It is good that it be published. The traditions of the Royal Air Force are recent, and, unless some permanent record is given to these magnificent achievements, only too soon will they slide into oblivion. The story will, I feel sure, interest both officers and men who worked with the Squadron in the war, and it will also hand on to the present and future members of the Squadron a record which shows great and daring deeds and a high conception of duty.

Part 1: Macedonia

CHAPTER 1

Outward Bound

The transport *Menominee* slipped quietly out of Devonport Harbour in the late afternoon of the 6th of September, 1916. Yet quietly is something of a misnomer, for, in addition to sixty officers and 2,000 men, the ship carried, stowed away in the heat of the hold, over 600 horses and mules. As the ship started, the horses set up an insistent kicking. The mules began to bray.

Among those on board who watched the receding shores of England were the officers and men of No. 47 Squadron, Royal Flying Corps. The squadron had been formed in May, 1916, at Beverley in Yorkshire, under Major F. G. Small; later it had a "zepp-strafing" detachment, first at Doncaster, and afterwards at Coal Aston, Sheffield, under Major J. H. Herring. At this time the squadron was used for training purposes, but in August it was mobilised as a Service squadron, and the personnel left Beverley for Devonport on September the 5th, embarking on the following morning. Major C. C. Wigram had command of the squadron, and with him as flight commanders were Major M. A. Black, "A" Flight, Captain J. W. Gordon, "B" Flight, and Captain A. Goodfellow, "C" Flight; Lieutenant D. F. Woodford was adjutant.

No one who travelled to the side-shows of the East will forget the journey. Accommodation was sometimes very bad; inconvenience, owing to the submarine menace, very great; but there were compensations. On some transports—the *Menominee* was one—the comfort of those on board was a first consideration. Just before midnight on the Sunday, the transport steamed slowly into Gibraltar harbour. The gaunt rock towered into the sky and the lights far up its side showed like stars. Presently a searchlight picked out the *Menominee* and held her in its uncompromising glare. Bells tinkled, and messages were flashed out. As the ship slowed to a standstill, the moon was released from a cloudbank so that the myriad harbour lights that had stabbed the darkness suddenly ceased to glare and softened into the landscape.

Monday was a day of rest. The weather was fine and the sky and sea were a deep blue. Some bathed from the boat's side; others lazed on deck enjoying the scene. The passing to and fro of boats; a gun high up on the side of the rock firing at targets made to resemble the conning-towers of submarines, which were being towed well out to sea; the purple hills of Portugal and Spain; Morocco looming far off with the snow-capped Atlas mountains grey against the horizon. Before breakfast next morning crowds of hucksters in small boats laden with cigarettes and fruit were importuning the troops from the side of the ship. At 9.30 a.m. the *Menominee* left Gibraltar harbour with its escort, and by the afternoon was hugging the African coast. At 6 p.m. on the following day, Wednesday, the boat was off Algiers. Before Tunis was passed there were rumours of mines and submarines, but nothing untoward happened and Malta was reached at 9.30 on Saturday morning.

This was September the 16th, and in the evening wireless news was received giving a brief summary of the previous day's advance on the Somme, and everyone was immensely cheered. Malta was left behind on the evening of Saturday, and land was not seen again until early on Sunday morning, when the island of Crete came into sight. In the afternoon, as the Greek mainland was approached numerous other small islands came into view. The *Menominee* had crossed the track attributed to the earliest of flying men. Maurice Baring has given us a fine translation of Phillipe Desportes' poem:—

Here fell the daring Icarus in his prime,
He who was bold enough to scale the skies;
And here bereft of plumes his body lies,
Leaving the valiant envious of that climb.
O rare performance of a soul sublime,
That with small loss such great advantage buys!
Happy mishap fraught with so rich a prize,
That bids the vanquished triumph over time!
So new a path his youth did not dismay,
His wings but not his noble heart said nay;
He had the glorious sun for funeral fire;
He died upon a high adventure bent;
The sea his grave, his goal the firmament;
Great is the tomb, but greater the desire.

Some of those on the *Menominee* were, like Icarus, to dare too much.

12

CHAPTER 2

Early Adventures

Salonika approached from the sea is like some fairy city. The *Menominee* steamed along the narrowing Gulf of Salonika in the afternoon of Tuesday, September the 19th, and every one gazed with questioning eyes at this new country. Mount Olympus rose clear-cut against the brilliant colouring of the western sky, and the bare, rugged hills encircling the city were mellowing with purple light. The town itself, apparently all fine villas and gardens and minarets, rose tier upon tier to the feet of the distant hills. But what disillusion awaits the traveller! The fairy trappings cover a multitude of rags.

The disillusion does not always come at once, for there is much of interest in this city which has had such a troubled past. In war-time there was the added interest of a very heterogeneous collection of rogues, heroes, and nondescripts of all nationalities in dresses ranging from those depicted in Biblical illustrations to the New York outfit of a be*fezzed* merchant; from the ample breeches of a Greek evzone to the practical shorts of the British soldier. The squadron marched to a rest-camp at Karaissi, a spot about 2½ miles north-west of the town, and remained there until transport came to take them to Mikra Bay on the following morning.

Mikra Bay was the home throughout the rest of the campaign of certain Allied air detachments which defended Salonika. It lies about 4 miles south of the town of Salonika, and was already occupied by No. 17 Squadron when No. 47 arrived. There was no accommodation ready, and on arrival the whole squadron were kept busy erecting tents and getting a camp made. The history of 47 Squadron is knit into that of No. 17. There was a close bond of sympathy between the two squadrons. On occasions they worked together, in composite flights from a common aerodrome.

The work of No. 47 Squadron will only be properly intelligible if we examine briefly the positions of the contending armies about the

SALONIKA FROM THE AIR, SHOWING BRITISH G.H.Q.

time that the squadron took the field.

In the Balkans the first shots of the war were fired and the first "cease fire" was ordered. The history of the campaign is one of intrigue, of the heroism of a little nation, and of the initial failing of Serbia's Allies, which was afterwards retrieved. Four times during 1914 the Serbs repelled invasion, and, after their final victory at the Battle of the Ridges in December of that year, compelled the Austrian forces temporarily to abandon the struggle. But the fighting had left the Serbian Armies weakened, and this weakness was accentuated by disease and famine in the summer of 1915. By this time, too, the situation in the Balkans had changed considerably. Turkey had come into the war and was badly handicapped at the Dardanelles for lack of munitions.

The Germans, who had not obtained the anticipated success against the Russians in the Vilna salient, turned to the Balkans, where, amongst other advantages, a successful advance against Serbia would free the Berlin-Constantinople railway and allow the sorely needed munitions through to Turkey. By the 5th of October, 1915, all was ready for the attack under Von Mackensen, and on the following day it was launched across the Save. In the meantime, Bulgaria was mobilising along the Serbian flank. On the day that the attack was launched, the British 10th Division had landed at Salonika, together with a French division from the Dardanelles. These divisions, inadequately clad and equipped, were rushed up to join the Serbs, but before a junction was effected by the British, the Bulgars, who had crossed the Serbian frontier on the 11th without any preliminary declaration of war, had swept across southern Serbia.

The remnants of the Serbian Army struggled through the snows of one of the worst of Balkan winters, over the Albanian hills. The British and French divisions retreated towards Salonika, but the Bulgars did not follow beyond the Greek frontier. Venezelos, the pro-Ally Greek premier, had promised the cooperation of Greece, but his policy did not receive royal approval, and on the day the 10th Division landed at Salonika, Venezelos resigned, so that the Greek support came to nothing.

During the winter of 1915-16 considerable Allied forces were disembarked at Salonika. In July, 1916, the reconstituted Serbian Army came into action again on the Serbian front and, in August, Roumania declared war on Austria. Now that Roumania had come into the war a general Allied offensive from Salonika was ordered, and in July the British pushed up-country and took over a stretch of line south

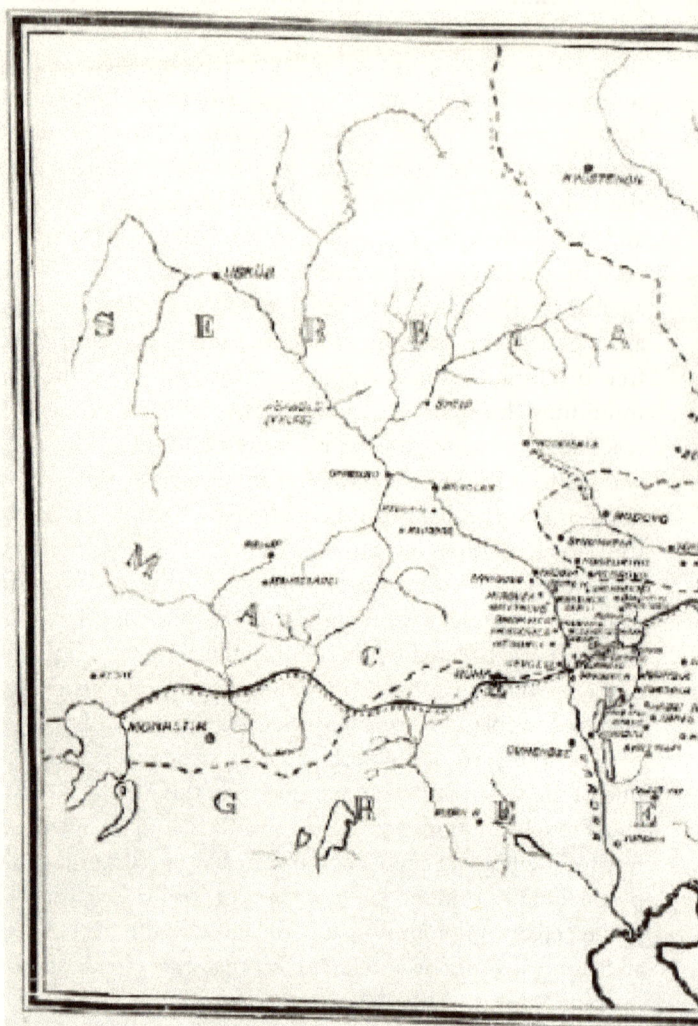

MAP
OF

MACEDONIA

SCALE OF MILES

APPROXIMATE ALLIED LINE

B U L G A R I A

SALONIKA

ÆGEAN SEA

and west of Lake Doiran. In the same month, No. 17 Squadron came to Salonika from Egypt to provide the indispensable aerial support. The British line in October, 1916, when 47 Squadron arrived on the Doiran front to commence active operations, ran approximately from the Gulf of Orfano to Lake Tahinos and thence south-west of Seres to Lake Butkova and along the Butkova valley to Dova Tepe at the foot of the Bela Shitza mountains. This, the Struma front, a hotbed of malaria, was held by the 16th Army Corps.

Between Dova Tepe and Lake Doiran, the line was held by an Italian division which later handed over to the 12th army corps, at this time deeply entrenched between Doiran Lake and the Vardar, where they had relieved the French. The stretch of line between the lake and the Vardar was the Ypres salient of the Macedonian front, not because it was a salient, but because of the constantly bitter and heavy fighting that raged along here, because of the heavy casualties, and because of the dominating enemy positions, the Grand Couronné and the Pip Ridge, which overlooked every movement that the British made. All the line west of the Vardar to the Adriatic Sea was held by the French, Serbians, Russians, and Italians.

On the same day that 47 Squadron had arrived at Salonika, there had disembarked also the personnel of wing headquarters and No. 17 Balloon Section. 16th Wing was formed with headquarters at 110, Rue Reine Olga (a place of mixed memories), and Lieut.-Colonel G. W. P. Dawes was given command of the wing. Colonel Dawes was a pre-war pilot of No. 2 Squadron, with which he had mobilized in August, 1914. He had flown from Montrose, **via** Farnborough and Dover, to France, taking part in the Mons retreat.

When the personnel of 47 Squadron left Beverley to embark, they had come without machines or transport. The transport had preceded them by a few days, travelling via Avonmouth. In the result, not until early October did a boat arrive with machines, and these were landed on October the 2nd. Great difficulty was experienced in getting the machines off the barges owing to the absence of any sort of mechanical lifting gear; the machines had to be manhandled. Whilst the squadron was waiting for machines, a small detachment was sent to Avret Hissar to be attached to "B" Flight of No. 17 Squadron, and other officers (mostly observers) were sent to the army machine-gun school at Lembet for instruction in the Lewis gun. This was rather "*pour passer le temps*," for they all knew the Lewis gun thoroughly.

By the 11th of October all machines had arrived and the transport was in the harbour on the *Uganda*. By this time, too, reconnaissance was being carried out along the Vardar.

On October the 15th a reconnaissance was ordered of Drama, behind the Struma front. It was from Drama aerodrome that much of the enemy air activity on the Struma front emanated later, and many fierce fights took place over the aerodrome there during the course of bomb-raids. On this occasion nothing of great importance was seen. When over Drama the engine of the observing machine, in which were Lieutenants Churcher and Faull, seized up owing to lack of oil.

Almost immediately two front cylinders were blown off the 90 horse-power R.A.F. (Royal Aircraft Factory design) engine, and the propeller was damaged. Any possibility of making our lines seemed hopeless, but at long last Churcher made a landing at Chai-Aghizi, which was just inside the lines on the Gulf of Redina, and south of the Struma mouth. Immediately the Turkish batteries commenced to range on to the machine, and the pilot and observer had to seek cover in the trenches. Help was forthcoming from the Royal Naval Air Service and during the night the aeroplane was salved, dismantled, and taken to Stavros, whence it was sent to Salonika on a lighter.

The squadron indeed were not particularly lucky with their aeroplanes at this period, and each time a pilot went up to test his machine after it was erected, a certain amount of anxiety was reflected on the faces of the orderly room occupants. This anxiety was not unfounded. On October the 19th, Lieutenant Andrews was testing his engine; at 6,000 feet he was over Lake Langaza, which lies beyond the hills to the north of Salonika, when his engine failed. A forced landing was made near the lake on very bumpy ground, and as the pilot could not take off again, the machine had to be dismantled and taken back to Mikra Bay. Nor was this all. Later, Lieutenant Durtnall, with Lieutenant Daw as passenger, went up to test his machine. The engine missed badly as he was taking off, and when he was over the sea at 300 feet, it stopped altogether.

The only thing to do was to "pancake" near two ships in the harbour. French naval motorboats rescued the pilot and passenger, and the machine was towed ashore and made fast to the end of the jetty near the aerodrome. The aeroplane remained partially submerged all night, and when being taken from the water next morning, suddenly broke its back and fell into the sea. After salvage it was dismantled and brought back to the aerodrome. On October the 20th "A" Flight of 47 Squadron moved up country to Janes to take over the air work for

19

the XII Corps. A few days later Headquarters and "B" Flight arrived at Janes, and on October the 30th "C" Flight went to Kukus. The squadron was now ready to commence work in earnest.

CHAPTER 3

The Routine of a Corps Squadron

The spectacular part of war in the air is fighting in the air. The primary and the most important work of aircraft for the navy or the army is reconnaissance. Fighting in the air came along because it is an endeavour to blind the eyes of the other side. The corps squadron's duty is to provide the corps command with information of all enemy movements on the corps front to a depth of some 15 to 20 miles; to mark down the position of enemy batteries, dumps, strong points, etc.; to photograph these positions and the enemy trench systems; and to keep this information up to date. It is not enough that the positions be marked once and for all. In stationary warfare the immediate battle area has many changes of appearance, and an important part of the corps squadron's job is to watch closely for these changes.

The main work is observing for the artillery. A battery can be fired from the map. That is to say, the artillery officer can measure up the distance between his battery and the target on a map, and, after making certain allowances, he can give his fire orders with a hope that his shots will fall somewhere near the target. But without observation of the fall of those shots he may never know whether his ammunition has found the target. Ground observation, when it is possible, offers some advantages, for usually the observing officer belongs to the battery which is firing, and knows all about his guns; but often ground observation is difficult, since every attempt is made at concealment, and every advantage taken of the configuration of the ground.

The air observer, on the other hand, sees the ground spread out below him, just as it appears on the map, perfectly flat, without any distortions. With experience he can quickly see the fall of the shot and estimate its distance from the target within a few yards, and he can spot a direct hit without any question of doubt. He can range more than one battery on to a target if necessary. He can even range different batteries on to different targets during the same flight. Furthermore, he can take photographs of the target before, during, and after the shoot, for the battery commander to study.

The work of the corps pilot and observer is done under difficulties. Assuming (which is not necessarily the case) that the observer is conducting the shoot, he must first and foremost know something about the possibilities of the guns that he is ranging. He must know roughly the time of flight of the shell in the air, its trajectory, and the effects of its explosion. He must know the rate of fire, the number of rounds to be fired, and the time to be taken to fire them. He may be called upon to range for almost any type of gun or howitzer. In addition, he must know something of wireless telegraphy. He has in front of him in his cockpit a wireless transmitting set, and he must be able to send up to sixteen words a minute.

He must be a good map-reader, so that he can pick up his target without delay and without mistake, and once he has called up his battery and started off the shoot, he must concentrate his thoughts on to the target, watch each shot, and signal back to the battery its point of impact. He must pay frequent visits to the battery position to look for any signals from the ground. He must be cool. Other machines are always in the air about him, and they all look much alike. He must be able to distinguish friend from foe, watch for an attack, and, if attacked, use his machine-gun with accuracy.

But fighting is not his job. He has a sting, but it is a defensive one. Nor is his machine built for fighting. It is a flying observation post and must carry all the impedimenta of an observation post. The fighting machine, on the other hand, is simply a flying gun-platform, and, thus able to reduce impedimenta to the minimum, has the advantage of speed, rate of climb, and manoeuvring power generally. The corps machine, having to work at a convenient height for observation, is also at a convenient height for enemy antiaircraft fire. The conditions are similar for the pilot or observer. The pilot may conduct the shoot, leaving the observer to watch for hostile aircraft. In any case he must be able to do so, and, in addition, pilot the machine.

Wireless telegraphy was adapted to the use of aircraft in the years before the war. During the early days of the war of movement in France there was little opportunity to use it, but when the line began to stabilise on the Aisne, a few machines, fitted with wireless, attempted to range for the artillery. The signals then used would now be considered elaborate. Words were spelt in full. In 1915 the clock-code system was first used in France, and this afterwards came into general use.

The code has the merit of simplicity. The point to be ranged on is considered as the centre of a clock with twelve o'clock pointing true north and the remaining hours accordingly. Imaginary circles are taken as circumscribing the target at radial distances of 10, 25, 50, 100, 200, 300, 400, and 500 yards. These circles are lettered J, W, Z, A, B, C, D, and E respectively (during the war the lettering was Y, Z, A, B, C, D, E, F). The observer notes the fall of the round with reference to the imaginary circle and clock hours, and signals the result, for example J3, D8, giving the letter of the smallest circle inside which the shell falls. To shorten the messages the signal 0 (zero) is used instead of 12. A direct hit on the ranging-point is signalled OK.

Observers often took up into the air a photograph, or, failing that, a map of the target, with the circles drawn according to scale and the north point marked on it. This was found of great use.

In addition to the signals of the clock-code there were many general signals in use. A favourite one was Cl, which meant "Am returning to landing ground." One or two other examples chosen from many are:—

B Are you receiving my signals?

LL All available batteries to open fire (sudden attack or very favourable target).

KQ Are you ready to fire? (Now FR.)

GO Continue firing in your own time.

NF Guns firing in position at.

RUF Are you firing?

W Shot unobserved or wash-out (now U).

TNK Tank.

The squadrons and batteries had their own call letters.

In the comparative leisure and stability of stationary warfare, deliberate arrangements can be made beforehand, between the artillery and the co-operating aeroplanes, and frequent practice can be carried out. But the testing-point of co-operation is reached under the conditions of moving warfare, when fleeting targets are constant and ground communication between squadrons and artillery commanders interrupted. There must be arrangements to call up batteries on to a fleeting target. There must be signals to indicate the advance of hostile infantry from their positions. In a word, the business of co-operation is a matter for minute and detailed arrangement, and the observer must not only be thoroughly conversant with the working of these arrangements, but on him is the responsibility, in moving warfare, of choosing the targets.

Something of the difficulty of the ground over which the pilots and observers of No. 47 Squadron did their work may be gathered from the account of the Battle of Doiran in Chapter 6. Most of the hostile batteries were situated in deep ravines which were themselves diverse and rugged in character, and thickly overgrown with a low, prickly bush which made the question of camouflage a comparatively easy one. There were many dummy emplacements from which flashes were sometimes sent to deceive observers. But these flashes could often be spotted for the harmless things they were, since they seldom had the "punch" of the flash from the muzzle of a gun when a shell is actually fired. Further, an examination of the neighbouring paths would show often that they were seldom used.

It is hard to camouflage a well-trodden path. Many were the devices tried by battery commanders to deceive the air observer. Another drawback due to the nature of the country was the fact that the enemy anti-aircraft guns were generally stationed on the higher slopes of the Grand Couronné or the Pip Ridge, whereas many of his batteries were in the ravines at the bottom of these heights. He therefore not only had the advantage for his antiaircraft guns, but he could also often bring an effective and unwelcome machine-gun fire to bear on the aeroplane. The majority of the members of the squadron spent more of their flying time co-operating with the artillery than on any other form of flying activity. The work was trying, but for those actually doing it, it was also full of colour and the satisfaction of seeing results. The value of the work cannot be reduced to the form of statistics.

Aerial photography played a great part in the co-operation between artillery and aircraft. Every corps squadron had cameras for taking either oblique or vertical photographs, and a corps squadron was normally responsible for all photographic work in a counter-battery area up to a certain distance, which varied between 3,000 and 5,000 yards behind the enemy line. Beyond this area photography was usually done by army two-seater squadrons.

From a photograph one can learn a great deal about the positions of enemy batteries. Suspected positions can be closely studied on the photograph, and a careful comparison of old and new photographs of an area will unfold a story of work carried out often in the dark. Fresh work done on a position will show up, especially if time has not yet been found to camouflage adequately. New tracks tell many tales.

With each squadron there was, in the war, an artillery liaison officer. Those attached to No. 47 included Lieutenants Pirrie, Page, and MacDonald, at various times, and they all did great service. The artillery liaison officer maintained the closest possible touch between the squadron and the batteries, stretched over a wide front, for which the squadron observed. He arranged, in conjunction with the squadron commander, for new observers to be sent up the line to be attached to a battery for a few days. Whilst there the observer would possibly help to conduct from the ground a shoot with an aeroplane from the squadron. He would learn also the range and field of fire of the guns of the battery, and something of their work. He would go into the trenches and spend some time in a forward observation post with one of the officers of the battery.

Not a small advantage accruing from this arrangement was the friendship established between the Royal Flying Corps observer and the members of the battery. The observer, too, could explain to the gunners some of the difficulties and limitations of aerial observation. As a result of such a visit a "shoot" with that particular battery would be looked forward to with the keenest interest. The artillery liaison officer was a great friend to new observers. He was constantly studying the photographs. In 47 there was made a large model of the whole country between Doiran Lake and the Vardar. On this model the liaison officer would point out to a new observer the positions of batteries, and with the help of a series of photographs would give him many hints and much information about the ground.

Furthermore, he always questioned observers returning from flights over the lines, and from these discussions stored up knowledge that had not a little to do with the reputation for efficiency which No. 47 had among the artillery units on the front. Another contributing factor was the ability with which the squadron wireless equipment was handled. This was largely due to the wireless officer, Lieutenant M. C. Evans. A tribute to his popularity is contained in the fact that he was known to everybody as "Dusty," but, unlike Daudet's philosophers, he was always uncommonly well groomed.

The value of photographs is not restricted to their use in connexion with artillery co-operation. They are enormously valuable to the infantry and other arms, more particularly for an attack. Photographs, both oblique and vertical, were distributed down to companies of a battalion, and the troops making the assault were able to study minutely the ground over which they were to attack. From the aerial photographs, too, whole maps were made up. This was a great boon. The maps in existence when the Royal Flying Corps arrived in Macedonia were so misleading as to be almost useless. From the photographs the maps showing trench systems, etc., were constantly brought up to date.

In France the corps squadrons were protected by army squadrons equipped with special fighting machines. These carried out offensive patrols well behind the enemy lines, thus keeping him too busy to concern himself with the destruction of the corps machines. In Macedonia things were different. Each squadron had to provide its own protection, and for this reason there were always a number of scout machines in the squadron, which were used for escort purposes. Later "A" Flight was equipped with scouts and did the work of a fighting squadron.

So much for the broader aspects of the duties of a corps squadron. What the duties were in detail, so far as 47 is concerned, will, it is hoped, be clear from the account which follows.

CHAPTER 4

The First Winter

Janes can hardly be called a town. Possibly it was one of the thriving communities wiped out during the Balkan Wars. Macedonia is dotted with derelict villages left behind by the flood of those wars. There is nothing now standing to mark where many of the villages stood, for the stones were taken from their ruined walls to metal the roads used by the British armies.

Janes consisted of a railway station, and little more. Up on the hills behind the station, where the XII Corps had their Headquarters, there was an ornate church (where once the Bishop of Birmingham preached to the troops) and a few houses; otherwise, the interest of Janes was wholly military. It was a dump for the divisions operating on the Doiran front.

The aerodrome was near the railhead, and was situated outside the quaint village of Armutei. Usually, the village was deserted, and in the spring crowds of storks settled down in every tree and on every chimney-pot. It was a spectacle, watching the young ones learning to fly. They seemed always to choose the bumpiest part of the day, and, after lunch, there would be hundreds of them in the air by the side of the aerodrome, indulging in all manner of aerobatics. Sometimes they crashed out of control. Soon after the squadron settled into the aerodrome at Janes, a stork was adopted, and a spare-time occupation of the pilots and observers was to collect frogs for the stork's food. It waxed fat and Macedonian.

On November the 1st, the squadron received its first visit from a hostile bombing machine, which appeared over the camp at noon, flying at about 9,000 feet. Three bombs were dropped, doing no damage, and Captain Goodfellow gave chase on a Bristol scout. The German biplane was caught up over the lines near Guevgueli, and Goodfellow gave the enemy half a drum of ammunition. The range was, however, too great, and there was no result. The biplane dived steeply to its

27

aerodrome. Goodfellow had bad luck a day or two later when his gun jammed as he opened fire on an enemy biplane from 50 yards. This machine was one of a formation which had raided Salonika; it was amusing to see the Armstrong-Whitworths (A.W.'s) climbing laboriously in a vain endeavour to reach the height of the enemy.

On November the 12th, Goodfellow on a Bristol scout went up to search for hostile machines which had been reported over the lines. He climbed above the clouds and headed for Guevgueli on the right bank of the Vardar. The loneliness of the scene was soon broken by the appearance of the enemy machines. They were three: a Fokker, an L.V.G. (*Luft Verkehrs Gesellschaft*), and an Albatross. Choosing the Albatross, Goodfellow dived, holding back his fire until he was close up. The Albatross dived away straight through the clouds and did not again appear. Then for some minutes a hot fight ensued with the other two machines, and after the Bristol scout had fired some three drums, the hostile aeroplanes gave up the combat and dived down through the clouds, followed by Goodfellow. The enemy machines were last seen going down to their aerodrome at Hudova. In these early days Buckingham, Wilkinson, and Goodfellow (pilots), and Dale, Mather, and Wilson (observers) all did excellent work.

2nd Lieutenant D. J. Taylor, who left 47 Squadron for Egypt in November, was an early casualty. He was killed on the 29th of December, 1916, in a flying accident at Abbasiya. His loss was much regretted in his old squadron.

In November, the squadron had a first taste of severe Balkan weather. No one who was on this front will forget the Vardar winds, which blew for at least seventy-two hours and were bitingly cold in winter and dust-laden in summer. They sprang up suddenly, and as suddenly died down again, and when they began any tent or hangar not properly put up soon found its way to the ground. Flying in this wind was difficult, but it had to be done at times. On one occasion Lieutenant Brooks, an observer with the detached flight at Kukus, lost his Lewis gun overboard as the result of a very bad 'bump,' which will give an idea of the violence of these disturbing concomitants of flying over mountains in a Vardar wind. One sometimes had to hang on like grim death.

In mid-November, Lieutenant Pirrie, M.C., R.F.A., was attached to the squadron as a gunner liaison officer. He had been preceded by Captain H. Sinclair Tait, the medical officer, who arrived on the 14th.

Whenever the weather was favourable, machines were fully occupied on reconnaissance, artillery co-operation, and photography, and the Bristol scouts had many fights with hostile aeroplanes. On November the 26th, an aeroplane despatch-letter service was opened between Salonika and XII Corps Headquarters. This was most useful owing to the slow means of ground communication between the two places.

On November the 27th, the infantry were pushing in the direction of Krastali, and, although the clouds were from 2,000 to 3,000 feet all day, which meant that they were not much above the summit of the Grand Couronné, constant patrols were kept up in order to assist the infantry. The presence of an aeroplane over the batteries had a disturbing effect on their fire. Getting guns into position far up the side of a pathless ravine is a long and difficult business, and battery commanders were consequently not desirous of moving their position too often. If, however, they fired so that their flashes could be noted by the observer in our aeroplane, they knew that in a short space of time their position would be pounded by our guns. Hence their preferred discretion when aeroplane patrols were up all day. In addition, the patrols kept off hostile machines from troubling the movements of our men.

The anti-aircraft fire which the Bulgar brought to bear over the area of the Grand Couronné was effective, and the presence of an aeroplane soon resulted in the sky being sprinkled with dirty puffs of smoke, for the enemy mostly relied upon high explosive. The shrapnel which we favoured burst with a clean, white, woolly puff that looked more picturesque than menacing. Seldom did a machine return to the aerodrome at Janes without a series of holes made by anti-aircraft shells. Usually, they were easily reparable. Occasionally a longeron was shot through or damage done which necessitated the attention of aircraft park at Salonika.

2nd Lieutenant J. B. Ackroyd, with 2nd Lieutenant E. E. Wheatley as observer had his aeroplane very badly hit during the course of a patrol over Doiran, but was able to return and make a safe landing.

On November the 29th, instructions were received for "C" Flight at Kukus to go to Snevce, and the major part of the flight moved thence on December the 4th. The British were at this time taking over from the Italians on the hilly, wooded front from Popova above Lake Doiran, on the opposite shore to the Grand Couronné, and stretching away to Lake Butkova. This range of hills was confronted by the blank wall of the Beles mountains, and in the valley between the two the

Salonika-Constantinople railway followed a rusty and moss-grown course. Fighting here was all patrol work. Snevce is behind this front and the aerodrome was prettily situated.

Both Snevce and Kukus had been previously occupied by the French. Soon after the flight left Kukus, the field that was the aerodrome was being cultivated for tobacco. Thence afterwards one might see, depending from upper windows in Kukus High Street, long strings of tobacco leaves drying. Everyone seemed to cultivate a tobacco allotment. Kukus High Street was a steep, narrow place of undulating cobbles and looked like an eastern bazaar. Supplies to vary the rations for the troops up-country were often a matter of difficulty, and the rumour that Kukus had some newly arrived radishes or lettuce spread like a fire on the Janes plain in midsummer, and all roads led to the town. Green-stuff was a rarity.

No. 47 Squadron, as we have seen, was part of the 16th Wing, which in turn was one of the scattered units of the Middle East Brigade. This brigade, which was formed under General W. G. H. Salmond on July the 1st, 1916, embraced the R.F.C. units in Egypt, Mesopotamia, Salonika, East Africa, and Palestine. Only the aeroplane could make such a command possible. Although it included units separated by thousands of miles, the brigade was alive with a very real *esprit de corps* which was in no small part directly due to General Salmond himself. He visited all his scattered squadrons and chatted freely with the pilots and observers, many of whom he used to recognise immediately, although he had previously, perhaps, only seen them once at some training school in Egypt or similar place where they were one in a crowd.

On December the 9th, General Salmond arrived at the squadron headquarters and stayed two days. Before leaving he made an inspiriting speech to the officers and men, congratulating them on their work, which was done, he said, under great difficulties.

Reconnaissances carried out on the day of General Salmond's visit, over the area from the Vardar to Butkova, reported much of the country to be flooded. This meant that the infantry of both sides were having a gruelling time. On the following day, 2nd Lieutenant C. ff. Denning and Lieutenant J. R. Wilson (as observer) were on reconnaissance near Hudova when they were attacked by a hostile machine. Wilson replied to the enemy's fire and the enemy aeroplane was apparently hit. It, however, was eventually landed under control.

Lieutenants J. R. Wilson and C. B. M. Dale did some excellent work observing for the artillery on to a railway bridge south-east of

Guevgueli. This was undertaken to help the French who were demonstrating there, and the results included thirteen direct hits on the bridge, which collapsed on the south side.

Lieutenant A. L. Sutherland, with Lieutenant A. P. Adams as observer, attacked a hostile kite balloon, which was hauled down by a lorry at Furka. The Bulgar showed great anger at this attack, and a considerable number of "flaming onions" were thrown up at the aeroplane. The kite balloon and the machine remained none the worse for the adventure. The same cannot be said of the aeroplane which flew up from Salonika later in the day with the despatches. This machine made straight towards an A.W. which was on the aerodrome. The resultant collision totally wrecked the Armstrong and severely damaged the mail machine.

Three days before Christmas, Major Cyril C. Wigram said goodbye to the squadron and left for Salonika *en route* for England. Captain J.W. Gordon took over pending the arrival of Major F. F. Minchin, M.C., who came on January the 1st, 1917. Major Wigram had had a most busy and harassing time settling the squadron into its new aerodromes and arranging its work, and it was unfortunate that when everything was working most efficiently, he should have to go.

On the day that he left, two machines which were on a reconnaissance to Hudova had an unusual experience. They contained 2nd Lieutenant H. J. Gibson with 2nd Lieutenant A. P. Adams (observer), and 2nd Lieutenant W. H. Farrow with 2nd Lieutenant F. C. Brooks (observer), the latter machine acting as escort. Over Hudova, at a height of 10,000 feet, a hostile biplane was observed a short distance below. Both of our machines dived. Farrow and Brooks were well on to the tail of the enemy machine, diving at 120 m.p.h. (a little more might easily have been too much for this type), when suddenly the German turned. A direct collision seemed inevitable. A second before the impact the German machine dived. The right wheel of the A.W.'s undercarriage struck the wingtip of the enemy's top plane, which crumpled up.

One drum was fired by Farrow at point-blank range before the collision, and another by Brooks after. The hostile machine disappeared into the clouds. The engine of the A.W. began suddenly to cut out, and a course was steered for Snevce, the nearest aerodrome. Over Rabrovo two more enemy machines were encountered and engaged at long range. They, however, made no attempt to interfere with the course of the British machine. Over Furka it was subjected to violent fire from "flaming onions." Farrow made a good landing at Snevce.

On the following day, Captain W. D. M. Bell, when returning from bombing the enemy observation balloon at Furka, was attacked from behind by an enemy machine. Bell was on a B.E.12, (Blériot Experimental—a tractor biplane designed at the Royal Aircraft Factory; the number refers to a variant of the type), a good single-seater machine of which a few had reached the squadron in November. As the hostile machine went under him, Bell dived with engine full on and fired twenty rounds from 50 yards' range. The enemy dived and then began to spin. After a bit, one of the planes broke off and fell away and the machine crashed in "no man's land" just north of Selimli.

That night an infantry attack took place, and the following day a new use was discovered for the aeroplane, when Sutherland and Adams flew low over Lake Ardzan, at times almost touching the water, in an endeavour to put up the ducks for a sporting brigadier-general from XII Corps. There is no record of the bag.

Christmas Day was fine. Greetings were dropped on to the German aerodrome at Hudova, and a message condoling with the airmen about Bell's victim of a day or two before.

Boxing Day passed, and then on the following evening there sprang up another Vardar windstorm. The Vardar wind bites through to the marrow. The whole squadron were called out to rush from tent to hangar rectifying any temporary advantage gained by the storm, and by their efforts damage was kept at a minimum.

On January the 1st, 1917, Major F. F. Minchin, M.C., took over command of No. 47 Squadron.

A bomb-raid on the enemy aerodrome at Hudova had been planned to take place in the last days of 1916, but the weather stopped this from being done until January the 5th, 1917, when eight bombing machines left with twelve 20 lb. and five 100 lb. bombs. The machines, despite difference in type, kept good formation, and the dumps and camps were hit and one camp set on fire. The station was hit and one of two sheds destroyed. The formation was led by Captain Goodfellow, and among those who took part in the raid was Major Black, who had only just returned to the squadron from Egypt. 2nd Lieutenant A. D. Pocock failed to return. He was seen to go down near Guevgueli on the enemy side of the lines, probably owing to engine failure, and as the formation left the lines it was seen that Pocock had set fire to his machine. There was a little fighting, but with no loss to the enemy, and at the expense of two flying wires on Captain Bell's machine.

This was Captain Goodfellow's last raid with 47; two days later he left Salonika for Egypt.

The weather hereabouts remained poor until January the 14th, which broke with the mountains rising clear-cut against a cloudless sky—a winter day of sunshine such as one gets only in Macedonia, or the high Alps, when suddenly the most distant hills are seen clearly as through powerful glasses, and details are sharp-cut on the mountain-side. Consequently, there was great activity, which was welcome after the muddy stagnation of the past few days. The artillery co-operation was repeatedly hampered by the presence of hostile machines. The batteries from time to time had to take in their ground-strips so as not to reveal their positions to enemy observers. A message was dropped on Hudova aerodrome asking for news of Pocock, and at the same time news was given of captures made by the French.

The morrow, which broke misty, soon cleared to a brilliant day; it was as though during the night some giant stage-manager had taken the range of the Beles and had advanced them many miles until they loomed against the aerodrome. Sometimes they seemed far off as they lay shadowed in the distant mists; at other times, for all their 15 or 20 miles, they appeared to enclose the end of the aerodrome, like the wall of a Turkish *harem*, implacable, complete.

There were two casualties during the day. Major Black, with 2nd Lieutenant A. P. Adams as observer, and Lieutenants S. J. M. White and H. Matthews had set off on reconnaissance to Hudova and Petrich. When nearing Petrich, White was attacked by two enemy machines, and before Major Black could offer assistance, White, who must have been hit early on, was diving steeply, apparently out of control, closely followed by the two enemy machines. The British machine—an Armstrong-Whitworth—dived sharply into a pine forest on the steep slopes of the Beles. Two days later a German aeroplane flew over the aerodrome at Snevce, and after dropping bombs to attract the attention of the Flight, let fall a message which read as follows:—

The Royal Flying Corps.
The German aviators are very sorry to inform you of the death of the two English aviators which were killed on the 15th January 10.30 a.m., after a fight with our aeroplanes. The English aviators had been fighting very bravely, but their aeroplane dropped after about 5 minutes fight and 'skilled.' They died as heroes, and have all our respects. Their bodies will be buried

with all military honours.

We are informing you also of your Lieutenant Pocock having been made a prisoner by the troops without being blessed.

We are obliged of your having informed us of the four German aviators which have been made your prisoners.

The German Flying Corps.

The German officer who wrote this message was probably quite unconscious of the humour of the second paragraph; his English rendering of the French word for wounded would, to Pocock anyway, seem to be equally apposite.

On this same day Adams was responsible for a clever piece of work. Piloted by 2nd Lieutenant R. E. Buckingham, he was about to begin a shoot on a hostile target in co-operation with one of our own batteries, when he noticed that there were ground-strips out on the enemy side of the lines. He at once sent down certain enemy signals which were known to us, and the hostile battery began to fire, enabling Adams to mark down the exact co-ordinates of the position. The 138th Siege Battery was later ranged on to these guns. Lieutenant Adams later on took his wings and worked with No. 30 Squadron in Mesopotamia, where he died fighting.

On January the 19th, the first enemy machine shot down by 47 in the British lines fell to 2nd Lieutenant C. ff. Denning. Denning, when acting as escort to a reconnaissance machine, met it over Kilindir. He was on a B.E.12, which at its best would do about 95 m.p.h. The German machine was a 2-seater Albatross with 200 h.p. Benz engine capable of well over 100 m.p.h., so that the Germans were in an easy position to escape by using their extra speed. However, Denning got above and behind the Albatross, and dived, firing one burst. The enemy observer opened fire with the rear gun, but the first burst from the British machine appeared to damage the controls, for the enemy machine commenced to spiral down. Denning followed, firing down to 700 feet, when escape for the Germans was impossible, and he therefore let them land 14 miles from Kilindir.

As he landed beside them, the two German airmen approached him, warning him off their machine, which was on fire. Denning rushed to the Albatross and put out the fire, which had done little damage. The machine was dismantled, and an examination showed that, in addition to shots in the fuselage, the base of the right-hand inner rear strut had been shot away, as well as the aileron control. The dismantling was done under shell fire.

On January the 27th, "B" Flight moved from Janes to Snevce and "C" Flight changed from Snevce to Janes.

The weather during the first half of February was consistently bad, and living was miserable in the knee-deep mud. Even the old Decauville line, that used to snort past the aerodrome on its way to the divisional dumps, ceased from snorting for a few days owing to dilapidations on the line. A steam roller that had been imported from England and was ambling across Macedonia bound on some swift and secret mission was overtaken by the rains and subsided into the receptive soil. It may be dug up at some future date and exhibited as an engine of war used by Alexander the Great. Little work could be undertaken, and when our machines did recross the lines a considerable part of the enemy territory appeared to be under water. As soon as the weather cleared a little it was seen that many alterations and additions were made to the front-line defences. These were reported on and photographed so that the maps could be brought up to date.

On February the 9th, thick black clouds were covering the whole countryside with snow, but the following day was a perfect winter day, with a hot sun, and the mountains, which everywhere had a fresh white coating, looked impressive. That night there was to be an attack by the Devons on the Petit Couronné across the sinister Jumeaux Ravine, now heavy with floods and snow. All day long our machines patrolled over the area, registering our batteries and keeping down enemy fire. All night the guns rumbled, and the black of the northern sky was constantly punctured by bright lights that appeared above the Jumeaux Ravine and then dropped quickly to earth. The attack over the snow must have been a weird sight. Once again, the men of Devon fought valiantly.

On the following morning, as four of our machines passed over to the west of the Jumeaux on their way to Hudova, all was quiet, and there were no signs, apart from the churned state of the ground, to show the doings of the night. Not that the pilots had much time to give to the ground, for they were occupied with the work in the air. Hudova was to be bombed and stiff opposition was expected. Furthermore, four of the machines which had started out had been compelled to return, mostly because of engine failure, before the lines were reached, leaving four A.W.'s and one B.E.12 in the formation.

It might be well to explain here what it meant to bomb in an A.W. This machine was designed chiefly for reconnaissance. A medium-sized two-seater biplane fitted with a 90 h.p. R.A.F. engine, it took about 40 minutes to reach 10,000 feet with a service load. At this height the machine had a speed of about 65 m.p.h. It was naturally a rather heavy machine on the controls, and although it was possible to do "aerobatics," all manoeuvring took time. With an observer in the rear seat the A.W. could always be expected to give a good account of itself.

When used for bombing, an observer could not be taken owing to the weight of the bombs, and consequently the pilot of the A.W. felt a little uneasy as to the protection for his "tail." However, bombing had to be done, and these were the only machines to do it. The four machines reached Hudova, where they were heavily attacked. Despite this, they persevered to the objective, and all bombs were dropped without observation of the results, owing to the violence of the enemy fire. Lieutenant Denning, who was escort on a B.E.12, had three fights in succession, and in two of these he seems to have driven his opponent down. Major M. A. Black was attacked over Hudova aerodrome by a Fokker, and was last seen going down in a spinning nose-dive, closely followed by the German machine. The enemy wireless two days later contained the following:

> East of Hudova, Lieut. Ebranecke shot down an English biplane, which was completely smashed by its fall. The pilot is dead.

The A.W. was also used for contact patrol. It was indeed a general-utility machine. On February the 17th, Captain J. W. Gordon, with Lieutenant E. E. Wheatley as observer, when carrying out a contact patrol over the Brest area, descended to 200 feet and opened fire on a party of Bulgars. Three dives were made, and on each occasion the enemy lay down and opened rifle fire on the machine. Whilst making further searches for hostile infantry the A.W. came down so low that the wireless aerial got caught in the scrub and was broken off.

Then came the German bombing squadron, and a period of great activity for the Royal Flying Corps in Macedonia.

CHAPTER 5

Gothas!

There is no reason why I should call this chapter "Gothas," for there was only one Gotha in the party. Yet to the majority of soldiers in Macedonia they were Gothas, and that perhaps is sufficient reason. Actually, the squadron, No. 1 *Kampf Geschwader*, which had been brought over from Bucharest, consisted of eighteen machines made up of Halberstadt scouts with 120 h.p. Mercedes engines, A.E.G.'s (*Allgemeine Elcktrizitäts Gesellschaft*) with two 220 h.p. Mercedes, Rumplers with two Benz engines, and Friedrichshafeners with two 220 Mercedes, plus the one Gotha. This squadron had been specially practised in formation bombing from the earliest days of the war and had distinguished itself on the western front.

Like a bolt from the blue, they first appeared on February the 26th. Twenty machines, flying fairly low and in superb formation, were seen to be coming down the Vardar from the direction of Hudova. Connecting up with the British line, but on the other side of the Vardar, was the French line, and behind this, but quite near the river, was the French aerodrome at a place called Gorgop. Before the French airmen could realise the significance of the oncoming formation, it was circling overhead and well-aimed bombs were falling. Eight French machines were destroyed and four damaged.

This was a serious loss, and in consequence the French were unable to continue the patrolling of their lines between the Vardar and Isvor, and called upon the Royal Flying Corps to give assistance. No. 47 Squadron received orders to extend their patrolling area in the direction of Gorgop. In view, however, of the very wide area allotted to the squadron, and of the fact that it was already overtaxed, no additional definite responsibility was undertaken. Before No. 47 learned of these things the presence of the bombing squadron was forcibly brought home to everyone at Janes. The enemy policy, a sound one, was to tackle the aerodromes first of all before attempting to destroy dumps at their leisure.

Having dealt with Gorgop in the morning, attention in the afternoon was turned to Janes, and soon after lunch they appeared. Most machines were got off the aerodrome before the bombs began to fall, but owing to their lack of speed they were unable satisfactorily to engage the enemy, and pilots and observers, as they climbed laboriously upwards, were able to look down on the aerodrome and watch some forty bombs bursting around the hangars and tents. Soon the whole place was covered in smoke, and when it cleared anything might be expected. As it happened, however, most of the bombs had fallen in a line just outside the hangars and no great material damage was done.

Everything was punctured with holes, and at night when lights were burning it was as though thousands of minute lanterns were hung about the camp. The toll in life was greater. Seven men were killed and Lieutenant E. McM. Howes, the equipment officer, and eight men were wounded. The mechanics behaved admirably. They were a splendid lot of men, and those that were killed were among the best in the squadron, which was also unfortunate in losing the services of Lieutenant Howes at a time when his valuable experience was sadly needed. The men worked far into the night, tuning up the machines, suggesting improvements here, altering rigging there, to make them their best to receive the enemy on the morrow.

On the morrow they came. It was a common sight to see flights of duck and geese flying overhead in V-shape formation on their way to the lakes and wild marshland, that string across Macedonia. The formation of the bombing squadron as it appeared over the hills was wholly similar, and at first might have escaped notice but for the ominous hum of the engines. As the machines came nearer they lost their aspect of wild duck and looked, to quote one observer, "like cathedrals flying through the air."

On this day, however, the bombers passed to the west of the aerodrome, heading southwards for Salonika. They numbered twenty, and on arrival at Salonika were attacked by the seven available machines of No. 17 Squadron and, despite superior numbers, the formation was broken up and one Halberstadt scout was forced to land at Gumendze; the pilot, a Lieutenant Kaistner, was taken prisoner by the 122nd French Division. Salonika was, however, successfully bombed. Just north of the town was a base camp called Summerhill, where a very heavy number of casualties was caused. One bomb fell amongst a party of men who had come down the line to catch the leave-boat to England.

The machines of 47 were in the air waiting to intercept the raiders, who split up into small groups, and each machine of 47 fought some three or four of the enemy. It was a great fight. Over No Man's Land between the Vardar and the lake the enemy made a stand and the anti-aircraft shells of both sides were bursting amongst the machines, The aeroplanes of 47 were not good enough to settle the combat, and, although they inflicted some damage, the enemy were able to withdraw when they tired of the fight and by that time many of the squadron machines had been badly shot about, although no one was wounded.

On March the 21st, "C" Flight moved from Janes to Kirec. The village of Kirec lies along the road from Janes to Lake Ardzan, and those from Janes who used to visit the lake in the hot summer days for a swim found that Kirec mess formed a very pleasant half-way house.

It is not easy to give an idea of the activity that prevailed whilst the bombing squadron was operating from Hudova. It should be remembered that, although the area covered by this squadron extended over many hundreds of square miles, yet that area was sparsely inhabited, and, behind the lines at any rate, camps and dumps were scattered, and a few days sufficed for the main dumps situated on different parts of the front to be visited. Furthermore, so far as the R.F.C. are concerned, there were only two squadrons to carry on all the necessary corps work along a 90-mile front, to fight and endeavour to prevent the bombing squadron, as well as other enemy machines, crossing the lines, and in addition carry on counter-bombing. Since, too, Hudova lay opposite 47 Squadron's front, they may be said to have borne the brunt of this extra activity.

There is no doubt about the fact of the moral effect of bombing. It was estimated in France to be to the material effect as 20:1. The moral effect is borne by the people who are bombed, and these always call for help to their own flying men. How often during the war in a bomb-raid did one hear the query, "What are our flying men doing, not to stop them?"! It is a dangerous query, for it is apt to lead up to a demand for a dangerous policy, that of defence. The man who is being bombed likes to feel that our own men are having a hit back, and he is often only convinced that they are so hitting back if he can see it happening. He wants to see an enemy machine or formation attacked every time it crosses the lines, and thinks that the proper way to ensure this being done is to keep patrols over our lines waiting for the enemy. Anything done in the air behind the enemy lines is out of his view.

Those who commanded the Air Force saw most clearly that the only true defence is a vigorous offence, and although at times there were difficulties, and even not a little pressure from those not equally competent to judge, yet they never swerved from this policy. How justified they were is apparent from the lessons learned at Verdun. Here the French adopted from the outset a relentless offensive policy in the air. Patrols were kept up far behind the enemy lines. German troops were attacked on the ground by low-flying aeroplanes. The moral effect on the German infantry and gunners was so great that they called loudly for defensive protection.

The phrase "air-barrage" (*Luftsperre*) was coined. There is a magic and a snare in catchwords. The phrase caught on, and henceforth the German airmen were largely used on patrols along and behind their own lines, with disastrous results. At the Somme, which followed on Verdun, the discomfiture of the German airmen was completed. The German air service went to pieces, and General von Hoeppner was called in to reorganise the whole service as an independent arm. Von Hoeppner recognised the great mistake that had been made in adopting the air-barrage policy. He at once set to work to copy the offensive methods of the British and French, and under him the enemy air service recovered its moral.

Those in Macedonia whose duty took them along on their two slow feet were no exception to the general rule, and occasionally one had to contend with an attitude which could be met, not by question and answer, but only by considerable propaganda. To the average soldier, all aeroplanes in those days were alike. He rather put them into a class by themselves, and, like masons, bricklayers, or chorus girls, he expected them all to dance to a certain definite tune. That a slow two-seater reconnaissance machine could not overtake and stunt around a single-seater scout seemed to him to argue a lack of initiative on the part of the pilot rather than the engine. These things seem trivial, but the flying man is the servant of the infantryman, and it is well that the limitations of aircraft be fully understood by those who use them.

On March the 4th, a combined bombing raid by Nos. 47 and 17 Squadrons was arranged against Hudova. Twelve bombing machines and six B.E.12 escorts set out in good **V**-formation and five 100-lb., five 20-lb., and thirty-five 4.5 inch converted shells were dropped, causing damage to hangars, camps, and personnel. On the afternoon of the same day nine bombing machines with five escorts bombed Cestovo, where damage was done to sheds, marquees, and tents. This was some sort of retaliation, perhaps, for the raid made that morning on Dudular dump near Salonika, when several bombs fell on hospitals, causing casualties amongst the sick and wounded. It is only fair to add that this area was most congested and great ammunition and supply dumps shouldered up against the hospitals.

A few days later a night raid was attempted on Hudova aerodrome. Whilst the machines were in the air the moon became overcast with clouds and observation was difficult. Bombs were dropped on the aerodrome, and one machine which failed to locate the hangars dropped a 100-lb. bomb on Cestovo dump. March the 12th was a similar day. A squadron of enemy aeroplanes bombed the approaches to Vertekop, and once again there were several casualties in hospitals and field ambulances, and two English nurses were killed. Vertekop is on the railway that runs from Monastir to Salonika *via* Florina. It is many miles away from the Doiran front and is situated in vastly different country. There were no British troops in this sector except for odd detachments, and the British hospitals worked for the Serbian Army.

Thirteen of our bombing machines, escorted by seven scouts, left, in retaliation, to bomb Hudova aerodrome, carrying fifty-four 16-lb., six 100-lb., and one 112-lb. bombs. Considerable damage was done to the aerodrome again, and a direct hit was obtained on a train standing on the line. As the formation approached, many enemy machines were seen to leave the ground, and our formation was heavily attacked; one of our pilots, 2nd Lieutenant D. H. Glasson, was seen to be going down low over the enemy aerodrome, closely pursued. He failed to return.

During that afternoon the aerodrome at Janes was raided. Most of the bombs fell wide and little material damage was done, although the tin huts which housed the officers, and some of the men's tents, were again freely punctured with holes. A message-bag was also dropped, and made a better mark. The message read:—

Royal Flying Corps.
British aviator shot today between twelve and one o'clock; shot in the stomach. More particulars will follow. Has just died.

No further particulars came in. 2nd Lieutenant Glasson, who came from New South Wales, joined the R.F.C. in February, 1916, and went overseas with No. 47.

The German bombing squadron proved extremely troublesome, and made special measures imperative. A fighting flight was formed at Hadzi Junas, near Janes. This flight was under the command of Lieutenant F. G. Saunders; and consisted of three B.E.12's of No. 17 Squadron, and one B.E.12 and two de Havilland scouts (D.H.2's) of 47 Squadron.

The navy were asked to co-operate, and the officer commanding R.N.A.S. ships and units in the Mediterranean was approached for help. This was at once forthcoming, and four Sopwith fighters and one Sopwith triplane were sent on March the 27th. Unfortunately, the triplane crashed on landing at Salonika and had to be returned to Mudros. We shall hear more of the naval detachment, but one fact may be noted here. Those of the R.N.A.S. were wedded to the navy. They spoke of wardrooms and gun-rooms, and flew on compass bearings. They were of course only too keen to help the R.F.C., but they were greatly exercised as to how to show to all and sundry that their ways were of the sea and not the land. They solved this problem in characteristic fashion. They grew beards. But they were lovable though unshorn!

Meantime, pending a reply from the navy, the arrangements for the composite flight were put into force, and met with almost instantaneous success, for, on the 18th, two hostile bombing raids were dispersed and driven back to their own lines. Nor was that all; an officer of No. 17 Squadron who had already distinguished himself drove down on the same day one twin-engined machine out of control and completely destroyed another which crashed in No Man's Land. The officer was Captain G. W. Murlis Green and his machine a B.E.12. This flight continued to have great success.

Some few days later, on March the 25th, the wing temporarily lost its Commander, Colonel Dawes. It happened thus. Colonel Dawes set out with the intention of visiting the wing commander at Mudros. When over the Athos peninsula his engine gave out and a forced landing was made on the shore near Riha Bay, a desolate, uninhabited spot with no communications to Salonika. His disappearance caused much speculation in the wing, and on the following morning a machine was sent to search Cassandra, Longros, and Hasionoros peninsulas for the missing pilot and machine, but owing to the fog the search had to be abandoned.

Later in the day another attempt was made, and this time Captain Hudson located the machine and came down low enough to see four Greeks pointing in a north-westerly direction. It was therefore assumed that the colonel had gone across the peninsula to Toronis Bay.

The navy were so advised, and a destroyer went in search, bringing him back to Salonika on the 27th.

On the following day the naval machines were in action against the enemy bombing squadron and drove them back to their aerodrome before they could bomb their objective, which was Snevce aerodrome.

The scouts belonging to No. 47 squadron used any spare time in practising, and as a result of this a curious accident took place about this time. 2nd Lieutenant J. L. Bamford, of No. 17 Squadron, was on a B.E.12, and, on his return to the aerodrome after a patrol over the lines, he engaged Lieutenant E. R. Wilkinson of 47 on a D.H.2 in a sham fight over the aerodrome at Hadzi-Junas. In the course of this fight, Bamford dived below Wilkinson and collided with the under-carriage of his machine. The tail plane and rudder of the B.E.12 were swept away, and the machine immediately began to fall in a series of spins, completely out of control. At some 5,000 feet above the earth the aeroplane turned over on to its back and retained this position until it hit the ground with one wing.

Bamford received nothing more than concussion, and, after being torpedoed when on his way to Egypt to recuperate, was back again flying within a month. Some few months later, however, he was killed, fighting heavy odds. Wilkinson landed his D.H.2 safely, that is to say that he himself was unhurt, but the D.H.2 collapsed like a house of cards when it touched the ground.

The month of April was eventful for the British Army on the Doiran front. There were rumours of a great offensive. There were other rumours of an offensive by the enemy, which, owing to the peculiar position of the Salonika Army, must have caused some uneasy thoughts. Certain it was that dumps had been increased, ammunition brought up in great quantities, and infantry reinforcements in the shape of the 60th London Division. All along the line there was a certain liveliness. Some looked longingly over the mountains that blocked the way to the north and wondered whether they were soon to see over the other side. The story of that offensive will be told in the next chapter.

Meantime no rest was given the enemy aerodrome at Hudova. It was raided night and day, the first big night raid being on April the 2nd, when an effective and noisy barrage, including searchlights and green balls, was put up by the enemy.

On April the 5th, the enemy bombing squadron raided Karasouli. The machines from the composite squadron went up in pursuit, but, owing to the proximity of Karasouli to the lines, were unable to prevent the enemy from bombing his objective.

2nd Lieutenant W. H. Farrow was wounded during a combat, and unable to write a report. It would, however, seem that before being rendered partially unconscious he brought down an Albatross near Bogdanci. Although Farrow made a good landing at Snevce, he was only semi-conscious.

On April the 12th, 2nd Lieutenant L. H. Stowell and Lieutenant J. J. Boyd Harvey left the aerodrome on a photographic reconnaissance and, when over. Stojakovo, the machine came under the usual hot fire from anti-aircraft guns. This was the worst sector of the front. A little later the danger-spot moved and spread to include the Pip Ridge and the Grand Couronné area as well as the various dumps which received the constant attention of our own bombs. When over Stojakovo, the A.W. was hit by a shell, the rudder control was severed, and the elevator controls nearly so. The machine fell from 8,000 to 3,000 feet before control was resumed with the pilot operating the lateral aileron control, and the observer pulling the tail skid wire. Sometime after this, Stowell went to Egypt to instruct. Boyd-Harvey, however, remained for many a long day, and, instead of developing a respect for Archie, conceived a growing contempt for that gentleman.

Somewhere about this time a hospital—No. 20 Stationary—had come up to Sarigol, and the rumour that there would also be some nursing sisters with it had spread to the aerodrome at Janes. In Macedonia, more especially upcountry, one never saw a member of the fair sex for months on end. One rather longed sometimes to talk to an English girl. Therefore, when the rumour as to 20 Stationary came our way, on the suggestion of Boyd-Harvey, some four of us went by tender to the hospital with the express intention of bearding the matron in her marquee and asking for an introduction to four charming nurses whom we might take with us to Snevce, where we had to collect material. It was of course irregular.

It all depended on the matron. We were shown to her marquee by an inquiring orderly, and there was a *mauvais quart d'heure* as we sat twisting our hats, wondering what was going to happen. I, for one, felt like getting up and rushing from the place. However, at last the matron came in with a dubious expression on her face. We introduced ourselves. The dubious expression changed to one of mystification. At last Boyd-Harvey suggested that we thought that the nurses never had a chance to see the countryside, and as the R.F.C. had a sufficiency of transport, perhaps a few nurses would like to borrow our tender for the afternoon. He obscured the fact that a necessary condition of the borrowing was our being allowed to ride in it. However, the matron—a charming lady—supplied this deficiency.

Four nursing sisters were introduced to us, and we started off happy, but awkward, in the direction of Snevce. We were warned to look out for General Milne who might be about that area, and who might also be expected to take a strong line if he saw nurses joy-riding with officers. We had an enjoyable journey along the Kukus-Snevce valley, and only just missed running into General Milne on the return. The nurses' white dresses were very marked, but General Milne's Union Jack floating over his car was perhaps equally so, or, maybe, we were trained in observation. Anyway, we apparently saw him before he saw us, and were able to pull the flaps across the front of the tender, at the same time exhorting the driver to give a smart salute as we passed. Both the flaps and the driver did their duty, but it was a trying moment. All this by way of reminiscence when writing of Boyd-Harvey, and now to our *moutons*.

During a raid by the enemy of advanced bivouacs of the XII Corps (on which the London Scottish could get reminiscent), 2nd Lieutenant F. W. H. Thomas on a B.E.12 attacked four enemy machines in succession and, obtaining a very good position under one, fired a drum from his top gun into the fuselage of the enemy from a distance of 20 feet. The German aeroplane staggered and then turned to the right, going down in a spinning nose-dive. Thomas followed for about 1,500 feet, but as the engine was oiling up and the enemy was putting up a heavy barrage, pursuit was given up. When last seen the aeroplane was at 2,000 feet and still out of control.

On April the 29th eight bombing machines of the R.N.A.S., under the command of Squadron Commander Smyth Pigott, arrived at Amberkoi. This was "F" Squadron, which had a nomadic and useful career about the Mediterranean. Its job here was to carry out a counter-bombing offensive on a large scale, and right well it did its work. The men on the ground behind the enemy lines must have been sorry the Germans ever started to bomb, for in the end they got far more than the German airmen gave. As a mark of the efficiency of the enemy's anti-aircraft guns it is significant that during the course of a raid by "F" Squadron on the aerodrome at Hudova, on the 10th of May, four of the machines were badly hit by anti-aircraft fire, but returned safely.

"F" Squadron went to Stavros on May the 11th, and to Marian on the following day, in order to repeat their bombing raids on the Struma front. Here some fifteen days later a most serious accident occurred at eleven in the morning. The only men in the *bessoneau* hangar at the time were killed on the spot, and there is no satisfactory account of what happened. The bombs with which the machines were loaded, pending a raid, exploded one after another, and, in addition to the four men who were in the *bessoneau* at the time and who were killed on the spot, four other mechanics and a private from the 10th Hants Regiment were wounded. Ten R.N.A.S. Sopwiths were destroyed and eleven Clerget engines. It was a serious blow, and it was important that the enemy should not know of it.

Consequently, elaborate precautions were taken to prevent the news of the accident spreading. This was not easy where the doings of the R.F.C. and R.N.A.S. were a topic of general conversation on the front. However, that it was effectively concealed may be gathered from the fact that many weeks later staff officers at the base were quite ignorant of the accident. Orders were issued that the accident was not to be discussed, and these were loyally complied with. The charred remains of the machines and hangars were removed and hidden in the bushes, and traces of the fire were covered over with earth, shrubs being planted on the bare patches to obscure visibility from the air. This accident ended the valuable help which the R.N.A.S. had been able to give.

On the morning of May, the 2nd Flight Sub-Lieutenant H. L. Gaskell and 2nd Lieutenant J. Watt, the latter of 47 Squadron, were returning from the lines, where they had been subjected to heavy gun-fire, when, at about 5,000 feet over the Hadzi-Junas aerodrome, the wings of the machine seemed to fold up and the aeroplane crashed to earth from that height and both Watt and Gaskell were killed.

A reconnaissance of the Hudova area carried out on May the 10th showed that the sheds and hangars close to, and south of, the railway at Hudova, had been moved, and the train was also gone. It was therefore assumed that the enemy Bombing Squadron had left the aerodrome for a destination unknown. Later, in point of fact, it was identified in Belgium.

A sigh of relief went up at its departure, more particularly because it meant a temporary cessation of the pyjama-clad run from tent or hut to a dugout, or a precipitate dash for machines.

OBLIQUE PHOTOGRAPH SHOWING "PIP" RIDGE

CHAPTER 6

The Battle of Doiran, 1917

The Bulgarian front between Doiran Lake and the Vardar was one of exceptional strength. To an observer from the centre of the line from which the Allied attack was to take place, the medley of broken hills forming his position baffles detailed description except at great length. There are steep hillsides and rounded hills.

There is little soil. The hard rocky ground makes consolidation of a newly won position difficult, and gives overwhelming advantage to the defender, well dug into trenches that have been the careful work of three years.

Deep-cut ravines divert progress and afford unlimited opportunity for enfilading fire. But in all the complexity of natural features the 'P' Ridge and Grand Couronné stand out in conspicuous domination.

The former, from a height of over 2,000 feet, slopes southward towards our lines, overlooking our trenches and the whole country south to Salonika. To its right the country dips and rises to a less sharp, but no less intricate maze of hills, that mount tier upon tier, from Petit Couronné with its steep and rugged sides, above Doiran Lake to Grand Couronne, itself little lower than the summit of the 'P' Ridge. The enemy had taken full advantage of his ground.

He was strongly entrenched in three successive lines, with communication trenches deeply cut into the rock, and roomy well-timbered dug-outs, with concrete machine-gun emplacements, and, on the crest between 'P' Ridge and Grand Couronne, with concrete gun-pits.

It was the key position of the Vardar-Doiran defences, and he held it with his best troops.

This is taken from Sir George Milne's despatch dated December the 1st, 1918.

It gives some idea of the strength of those positions which stared out across our lines.

Sir George Milne received instructions towards the end of February, 1917, to be prepared to commence offensive operations during the first week in April.

The nature of these operations was, so far as the British were concerned, to engage the enemy on the Struma front, and to the east of the lake, and at the same time to make an attack in force west of the lake.

Preparations for the offensive were completed by April the 8th, but, for various reasons, General Sarrail found it necessary to put off the attack until April the 24th, when it was launched after a bombardment of the hostile positions extending over several days. It became early apparent that the strength of the enemy artillery had been greatly increased in anticipation of the attack.

Not until early morning on the 24th were despatch riders sent out from XII Corps Headquarters to notify the formations concerned that zero hour would be 9.45 p.m. that same night. The Bulgar appears to have received earlier, but not altogether accurate information. A deserter of the 33rd Bulgarian Regiment gave himself up to the 22nd Division on the night of the 23rd, and, on being questioned on the following morning, stated that the Bulgars had been warned to expect our attack at 8 p.m. that night.

The news reached Sir H. Wilson, commanding the XII Corps, after breakfast, and he went across to see Sir George Milne. It was decided that the information should not affect the plans. The deserter also mentioned that considerable reinforcements had arrived in the Dedeli area.

These were, in fact, the 39th Regiment and part of the 58th Regiment, as was afterwards discovered.

Air reconnaissances throughout the day had little of importance to tell, although in the afternoon some 1,000 men were reported marching from Dedeli in the direction of Hodza-Obasi.

The attack was made in the following order from right (the lake side) to left (P.4½ on "P" Ridge).

Division.	Brigade.	Battalion.	Objective.	Reserves and Supports.
26th	79th Brigade (Brig.-General A. J. Poole) 78th Brigade (Brig.-General J. Duncan)	7th Wilts 12th Hants 10th Devons 7th R. Berks 11th Worcester Regt.	O.1 and O.2 O.3 O.4 and O.5 O.5½ O.6	8th D.C.L.I. in Brigade Reserve 9th Gloucester Regt. 7th O.B.L.I. Brigade Reserve
22nd	66th Brigade (Brig.-General F. S. Montague Bates)	8th K. Shropshire L.I. 13th Manchester Regt.	380, Mamelon P.4½	9th South Lancs. and 12th Cheshire Regt. Brigade Reserve

In addition, there were in reserve,

The 77th Brigade in reserve to the 26th Division.

The 66th Brigade in reserve to the 22nd Division, with one battalion holding the Whaleback.

The 67th Brigade in Corps Reserve near Galavanci.

The 8th Mounted Brigade in Army Reserve.

The objectives O.1, ("O" from French "ouvrage"—a work etc.,) were distinct enemy works. O.1 and O.2 lay across the precipitous gap called Patty Ravine. Over this the Wiltshires were to go before storming the strongly held positions. O.2 was connected up with O.3 across the Wylye Valley, which in winter emptied its waters into the Jumeaux Ravine. O.4 and O.5 were what one might call the Petit Couronné position. The ill-starred Jumeaux Ravine lay between the Devons and their objective. The Jumeaux also came between the Berks and Worcesters, and 0.5½ and O.6 on the Scabbard. On the left of the 26th Division, Hill 380 and the work called the Mamelon offered a difficult task to the 22nd Division, but their most formidable objective was P.4½ on the scarred red slopes of the "P" Ridge.

The day had been cloudy with a fresh north-westerly wind. In the evening the wind dropped. The night was still and very dark, with some clouds. The new moon gave but little light and set at 10.44 p.m. Occasional lights along the heights of the Beles on the opposite shore of the lake twinkled down through the darkness like stars. To minimize the effect of searchlights, star shells, and so forth, the troops taking part in the attack had been ordered to blacken their faces. As the men assembled for the assault, this fact gave rise to many grim jests.

At 4.40 p.m. in the afternoon the enemy had registered a barrage

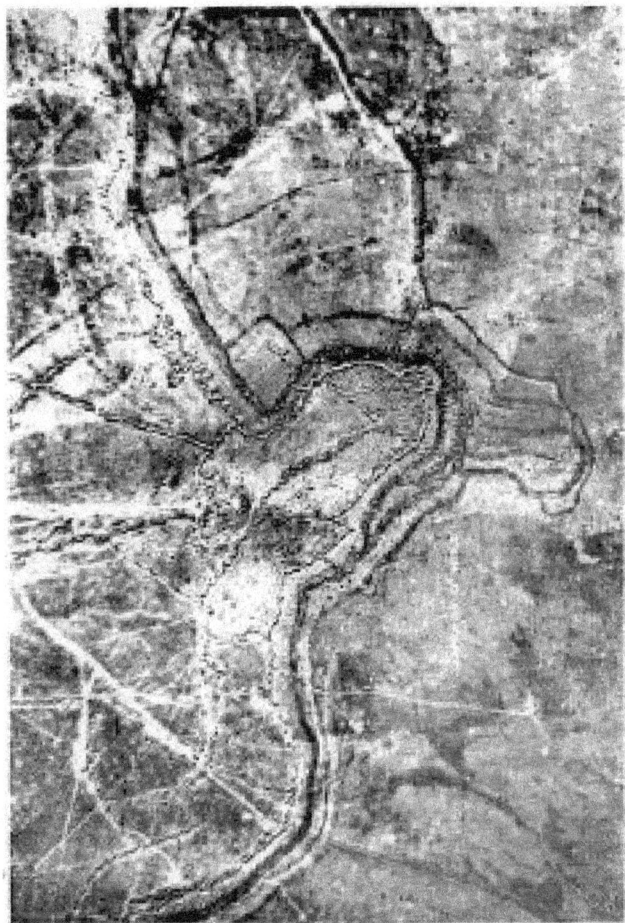

ENEMY FRONT LINE TRENCHES FROM THE AIR THE WIRE SHOWS UP PLAINLY.

in front of the 22nd Division, and again at 9.25 p.m. At 9.10 p.m. he put down a most heavy barrage along the whole front of the 26th Division. This was maintained throughout the attack. The heaviest part of this barrage was put into the Jumeaux Ravine, but both Wylye and Patty Ravines received their due share.

The 22nd Division gained all their objectives and were able during the night to consolidate the ground won, despite the fact that four determined counterattacks were made against P.4½. The total losses of this division for the night were 1 officer and 6 other ranks killed and 6 officers and 165 other ranks wounded. Four other ranks were reported missing.

The 26th Division were less successful. Over 50 *per cent.* of those who took part in the attack were killed or wounded, and, with the grey light of the morning, the division had completely withdrawn to our front-line trenches. On the extreme right, O.1 had been reached by one company of the Wiltshires with little opposition. The remainder of the battalion, caught in a murderous fire, failed to reach 0.2. Their losses were 14 officers and 313 other ranks.

The Devons and the Hants were caught by the barrage in the Jumeaux Ravine. The barrage consisted mostly of 8-inch high explosive and shrapnel. The noise and efficacy of the 8-inch shells, constantly falling within the confines of a narrow space out of which precipitous heights loomed vaguely, was magnified a hundredfold. Many casualties were caused before the troops had reached their assembly-points. The assaulting troops had to go across the Jumeaux before the real storming of the enemy positions could take place. The wonder is that any got across at all. Yet the right company of the Hampshires secured a footing on O.3; or rather a few of those who started reached their objective.

But they found the Bulgar awaiting them and inviting them on with a grim "Come on, Johnny." The survivors of two companies of the Devons, under their gallant commander Lieut.-Colonel T. N. Howard, got through. But by the time that reinforcements and ammunition reached them, the situation on either flank was such that the divisional commander decided that all troops should be withdrawn to our original lines, so the Devons were recalled. The few who got back brought with them 8 prisoners—7 Bulgarians and a German telephonist. This gallant battalion lost 16 officers and 402 other ranks. The Hampshires fared little better and lost 15 officers and 249 other ranks. The works on O.5 were never occupied. O.5½ and O.6 were taken, but given up in the withdrawal.

Through the cold, wan day of the 25th, stretchers were out bringing in the wounded, which the Bulgar allowed without any interference, even permitting stretcher parties right up to his own wire. At night the rain fell pitilessly.

During the following days the positions which had been captured by the 22nd Division were consolidated and arrangements made for a further push along the "P" Ridge. Before this could take place, instructions were received by Sir George Milne to postpone the operations, and May the 8th was fixed for the renewal of the Allied advance. The British were once again to concentrate their main effort in the vicinity of Lake Doiran.

The success of the 22nd Division in the original attack had created a marked salient, and it was therefore decided that the 26th Division should make a fresh attack upon the enemy's advanced position from Lake Doiran to the Petit Couronné. Meantime the 79th Brigade, which had suffered so heavily in the attack of the 24th/25th April, had relieved the 83rd Brigade to the east of Lake Doiran, and the latter had come into Corps Reserve. For the 79th this meant the taking over of a quieter sector. The left of this sector at Popovo was high above the lake, and many of the men who had taken part in the first attack were able to look down on the second.

In order to distribute as far as possible, the enemy's artillery fire, the 22nd Division was to simulate an attack against the line from Petit Couronné to P.4, and to advance its line to the west of the "P" Ridge opposite Krastali. It was also to send a small raiding force against the village. The 60th Division was to co-operate by advancing its line to Tomato Hill, Westbury Hill, and by occupying Goldies Hill. As a result of the experience gained in the first attack, it was decided to avoid the Jumeaux Ravine and to attack O.1, O.2, and O.3, and to occupy the Petit Couronné by a *coup de main* should opportunity offer.

The attack was delivered after a two days' bombardment, at 9.50 p.m., at moon-rise. The action of the 22nd and 60th Divisions was successful. The 26th Division fared hardly better than before. The divisional commander had received intimation from the commander-in-chief that the attack was to be pressed with the utmost determination. That this was done there is no shadow of doubt. Three Scottish battalions delivered the attack. The centre one, the 12th Battalion Argyll and Sutherland Highlanders, was the only one to reach its objective and commence the consolidation of the line. All the officers, however, were casualties, and as no supports were forthcoming, the troops fore-stalled heavy counter-attacks from front and flank by withdrawing. The casualties were some 12 officers and 210 men.

The 11th Battalion Scottish Rifles on their right were quickly enveloped in a thick cloud of smoke, dust, and mist, and it is hard to say what happened. They would appear to have become somewhat disorganised in the consequent confusion. The 10th Battalion Black Watch on the left were unable to penetrate beyond the enemy's front-line trenches, and when driven back made two further unsuccessful attacks, losing in all 10 officers and 370 other ranks. It was not until after 2 a.m. that the brigadier commanding the 77th Brigade was fully aware of the complete failure of his attack. He organised a fresh general attack at dawn, which was unsuccessful.

Meantime the 78th Brigade assaulted the eastern end of Petit Couronné (0.4) shortly after midnight. The 7th Oxford and Bucks Light Infantry, who delivered the assault, were met with an extremely heavy trench-mortar barrage, under cover of which the enemy made counter-attacks. Although all the officers except one or two subalterns quickly became casualties, this fine battalion repeatedly returned to the attack. Two companies of the 7th Royal Berks, sent in support, joined the remains of the Oxford and Bucks Light Infantry on the southern slopes of 0.4 after their second attack had failed, and Lieut.-Colonel Dene, commanding the 7th Royal Berks, who arrived later, assumed command. He organised a fresh attack, which was delivered at 5 a.m. after artillery preparation.

The attack was well led and vigorously carried out, and the extreme limits of O.4 were reached. The enemy immediately put his heavy guns on to the trenches which had been won, and this, combined with accurate trench-mortar fire, drove our troops back with very heavy losses. Colonel Dene's orders were to hold 0.4 at all costs, and, although wounded, when driven from the trenches he clung to the slopes of the hill with his few remaining men. Eventually, as the situation was an impossible one, orders were given for the withdrawal of the troops, and this was done with few further casualties. The 7th Oxford and Bucks Light Infantry lost altogether 15 officers and 447 other ranks; the 7th Royal Berks, 9 officers and 143 other ranks. So ended the battle.

From Doiran the activity moved to the Struma front and operations were in progress there when, on May the 24th, definite instructions were received from General Sarrail that offensive operations were to cease all along the front.

This, then, is a very brief outline of the first spring offensive in Macedonia. It may be argued that it has little to do with the history of No. 47 Squadron. No. 47 was a corps squadron, and as such was in close touch with the work of the ground units of the XII Corps. What manner of troops they were is evident from this survey of their attempt at the wellnigh impossible. The squadron took their part in these operations.

A secret order was issued from XII Corps Headquarters on the 18th of April dealing with the allotment of aeroplanes for artillery co-operation and close patrols for the forthcoming operations. This order stated that the fronts covered by Heavy Artillery Groups could, from the point of view of close patrol work, be considered to coincide with divisional fronts as follows:—

37th Group with 26th Division.
82nd "   "   22nd "
75th "   "   60th "

Before outlining the scheme of co-operation, the order set forth the functions of the various types of aeroplanes as follows:—

The "A.W." (Armstrong-Whitworth) aeroplanes are two-seated machines fitted with wireless and therefore available for artillery co-operation, carrying an observer.

The B.E.12 aeroplanes are single-seated scouting machines fitted with wireless and available for artillery co-operation, but without an observer and therefore unable to carry out detailed ranging.

The D.H. (De Havilland) aeroplanes are single-seated scouting machines, and not being fitted with wireless cannot carry out artillery co-operation. Distant patrols and contact patrols, the order went on to say, will be carried out, when necessary, outside the allotment.

It is unnecessary for the purpose of this history to set forth the detailed table of flights which accompanied the above order. It will be enough to say that a time-table was drawn up whereby machines were to be patrolling and registering over the front from dawn to sundown on each day of the bombardment. On the morning of the 23rd of April, the day before the attack, a photographic lorry was sent up to Janes with the necessary personnel, two enlarging lanterns, and stores

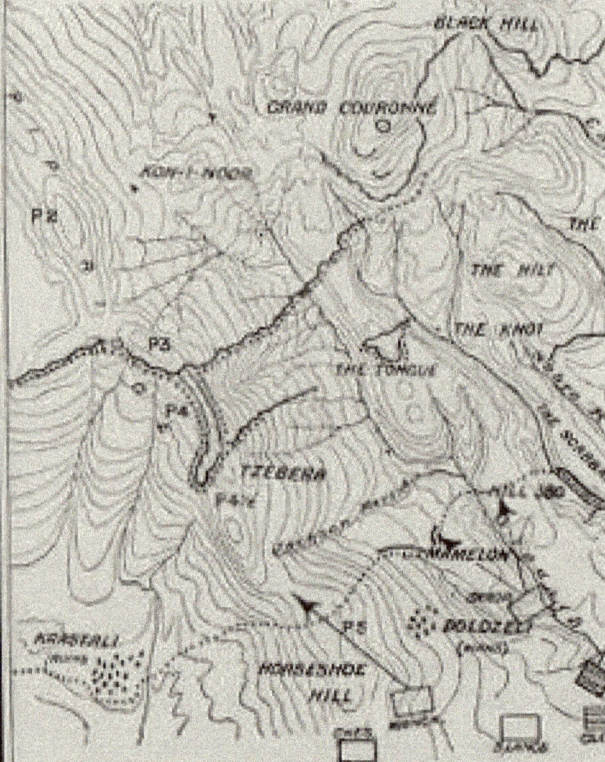

MAP
TO ILLUSTRATE

BRITISH ATTACK

APRIL 24/25, 1917.

SCALE OF YARDS

ENEMY'S MAIN ENTRENCHMENTS.

BLACK HILL

GRAND COURONNE

KOH-I-NOOR

P.2

THE

THE HILT

THE KNOT

P.3

THE TONGUE

P.4

TZEBERA

P.4½

HILL 680

MAMELON

P.5

BOLDZELI
(RUINS)

KRASBALI

HORSESHOE
HILL

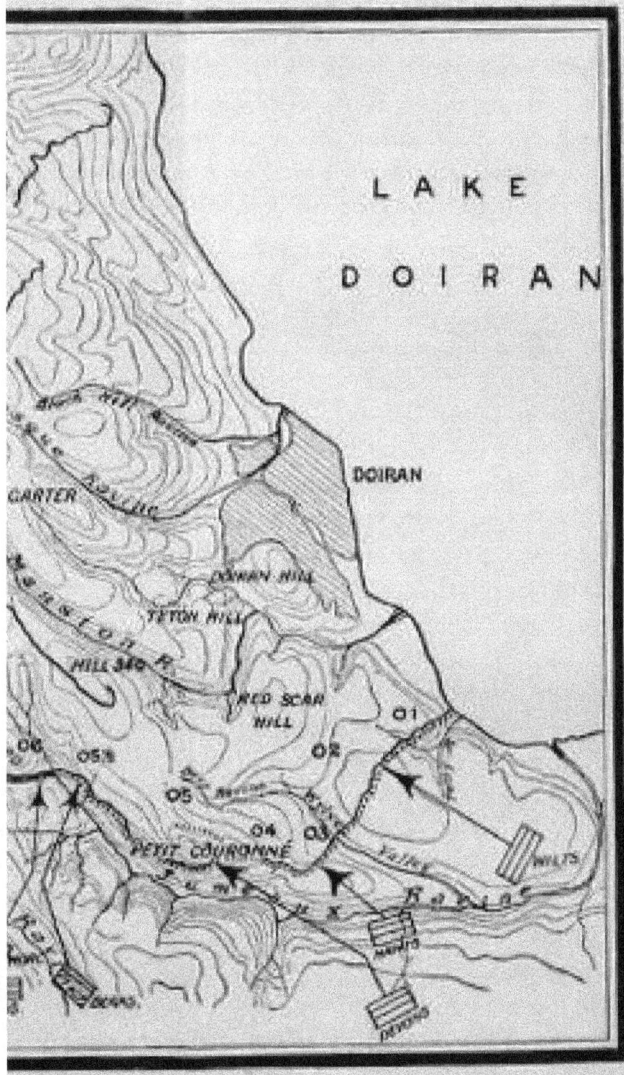

LAKE

DOIRAN

DOIRAN

BIRD HILL

CARTER

DOIRAN HILL

TETON HILL

HILL 340

RED SCAR HILL

O1

O6   O5½   O2

O5   O4   O3

PETIT COURONNE

WILTS

X

HANTS

DEVONS

available for about six weeks, for the purpose of developing any urgent plates which might be required during the operations. This arrangement was not, of course, sufficient to cope with any great influx of plates, but enabled urgent work to be done on the spot. Less pressing photography had to be done at Salonika.

Many records of No. 47 Squadron for this period are missing. It is therefore impossible to enter with any detail into the co-operation between the squadron and the artillery. Many destructive shoots were carried out on hostile batteries and, by their presence, the aeroplanes kept down retaliatory measures on our own artillery. As an example of the success of these shoots the following two instances are quoted from a 16th Wing summary. On one occasion, when ranging on a hostile gun-emplacement, two large explosions occurred—apparently an ammunition store was hit—and when the smoke had cleared away the emplacement had completely disappeared and nothing but a number of shell-holes was visible. On another occasion, three large explosions were seen and flames rose to a height of 400 feet. This again was probably an ammunition dump. A prisoner who was taken later referred to one of these shoots and stated that two guns had been destroyed.

There was no co-operation between aeroplanes and infantry in the attacks themselves, owing of course to the fact that they were carried out during darkness. By being compelled to deliver his attacks at night the British commander was deprived of attendant aerial support. It is true that the types of machines which 47 possessed were slow and much inferior to those flown by the Royal Flying Corps on the western front at the same period. On the other hand, they were well adapted for artillery spotting and most of the observers knew the ground thoroughly. The enemy had unmasked, to meet the attack, many new guns on to which aerial observation would have been of paramount use. Furthermore, apart altogether from attacks on hostile infantry and strong points which low-flying aeroplanes could have accomplished, contact patrols would possibly have eliminated the confusion of effort which took place.

Contact patrol had first been introduced on a definite scale by the British during the Battles of the Somme in 1916. Efficient co-operation between aeroplanes and infantry entails a very high standard of organisation, as well as very careful training of the Royal Flying Corps personnel and the ground personnel who are to carry out the attack. This training was out of the question for 47 Squadron, for the simple reason that there was never any time available for it. The Balkans were a subsidiary theatre of war, and the best had to be made of the material to hand. Despite all these and other drawbacks, had a dawn attack been possible the Royal Flying Corps could have given very material support. What the flying man can do against hostile columns during an attack was clearly demonstrated on this front in the autumn of the following year.

During the last week in May the following letter was received from the B.G.G.S. XII Corps by the officer commanding 47 Squadron:—

The corps commander desires me to convey to you, and to the officers and other ranks under your command, his great appreciation of the zeal shown by all ranks and the good work performed during the operations carried out by the XII Corps during the past month.

He realises clearly the strain imposed, not only upon pilots and observers, but also upon other ranks of the Royal Flying Corps in carrying out their duties at high pressure during a period of operations, and he has read with interest the reports rendered of the various flights carried out during this period.

CHAPTER 7

Summer Nights—And Gnats

The Macedonian summer has some fine, but many bad, aspects. Apart from the periods when the Vardar winds film everything, animate and inanimate, with fine dust, the weather can be relied upon to be consistently hot with fairly continuous sunshine. But the sunshine is bitterly paid for. The greatest torture came from the flies. The teachings of the nursery leave us with a benevolent feeling towards this most accursed of winged insects. As permeating as the dust, the flies recognised no place as sacred. They settled in their millions around the cook-houses and had high fun on every morsel of food through its various stages from its arrival at the base until its advent to the mouth. Some few even followed further. They tormented you every minute of the day. They knew of secret entrances to your mosquito-net. They retired late and were up betimes.

During their hours of rest, they were relieved by the mosquito. I could almost write a learned essay on the mosquito and malaria. I know in theory how to distinguish between the comparatively harmless *culex* and the malaria-carrying *anopheles*. I know by experience that they both bite. They used to come up to the hills from the marshy swamps of Lake Ardzan in clouds just as the heat of the day died down, and the western sky was a pure green, suggestive of an elusive peace. If the mosquito-net was proof against mosquitoes, then the sand-fly concentrated against it. On the morrow of a summer night, the man of sensitive skin was seen in a new light, his contours and colouring having undergone a decided change. The twenty-four hours of the day passed in a kaleidoscope of insects.

During the hottest part of the day, work not absolutely necessary ceased. This time was bad for flying, because of the "bumps," and because of poor observation due to the haze. A post-prandial rest was forced even on the youngest of the squadron, and it was during these uncomfortable hours of wet heat that snakes went abroad in search of food. The aspect of a long, sinuous, probably quite harmless snake curling its way across the floor of the hut in chase of a mouse that has eaten a hole through a best jacket is calculated to disturb the remainder of the afternoon's rest. The stuffiness of the Macedonian summer was tempered somewhat by the arrangements made by our P.M.C., Lieutenant L. P. Sedgwick. Sedgwick had grown up with the squadron. He organised parties to lay out a tennis lawn.

A corner of the aerodrome was chosen, and, for many odd hours, buried waist-high in the grass, to the joy of the large flies which, taking advantage of the fact that shorts were being worn, bit viciously and continuously, parties of officers might be seen scything merrily. At last, the necessary area of ground was ready. Oil was spread over it and stamped in in devious ways. The court was marked out. For a net one had to be content with rabbit wire run across between two stakes. Thus far, and a halt was called until the rackets and balls, for which a cable had been sent to Egypt, should arrive. There was no tennis *impedimenta* in the whole of Macedonia. Even Orosdi-Back at Salonika could do nothing.

After a delay which cooled slightly the first heat of enthusiasm, the rackets arrived. Thence for a few days the court was in full use. Until one night came the rain: Macedonian rain. The court was not washed away, but the rackets were. Carelessly left lying on the court, a treatment which they resented, they were of no further use. So ended, for the moment, the distraction of tennis.

But Sedgwick had other ideas. The mess, as were most of the officers' quarters, was built of wooden ammunition-boxes. Plans were drawn up for an addition to the mess. There was much whispering and much mystery. The officer in charge of the local ammunition dump was invited to the mess and treated as a royal and honoured guest. A few days later a load of boxes arrived. These were built around one corner of the huts. Time passed. There were bangings and goings and comings. Sedgwick, perhaps partly as a result of the excitement, fell sick of a fever, and the casualty clearing station at Janes opened a bed and received him into its cool sheets. To accentuate his isolation, barbed wire was put round his corner of the camp. Jones took over the task which Sedgwick had left incomplete. A tender going to Salonika was used to make sundry purchases.

At last the great night arrived. By kind permission of the colonel commanding, the famous band of the 7th Wilts came down to the aerodrome to play throughout the evening. Many illustrious guests were invited. The tender, which had stood outside the mess all the previous night, was gradually emptied in the direction of the new addition to the huts. A special dinner was put on. When the last machine came in from the lines and the whole mess were assembled, an unveiling ceremony took place. In what was the wall was now an aperture which disclosed a perfectly arranged bar with rows of multi-coloured bottles and the mess corporal in spotless white coat.

The bar was a great success. It was opened only in the evenings just before dinner. Ice was obtained fairly continuously from Salonika, and returning pilots and observers were not without gratitude for the long, cool drinks they could now enjoy. There was an unofficial guest at the opening ceremony. Some of us saw him hovering in the shadows, staring with satisfied eyes through the windows, beating time to the music of the band. He could still hear the distant music when, later in the evening, he looked out from his tent on the hill and wondered vaguely whether anyone had in the last hour or two visited in vain his contagious corner of the camp.

During the summer, flying duties were concentrated, so far as possible, into the early hours of the morning or late afternoon and evening. At these times the atmosphere was intensely clear, and the still, cool air made flying conditions ideal.

Throughout the month of June hostile machines showed considerable activity, crossing the lines at great heights, and reconnoitring the whole area down to Salonika. For this, and as a result too of the vigorous offensive kept up by 47 Squadron, the enemy withdrew machines from the Monastir front and concentrated them opposite the British sector. The possible explanation of this reconnaissance activity was the fact that heavy movements and changes were being made in the disposition of our troops. As, however, the enemy during this period made night flights over the area, it was considered that the gradual concentration of aircraft on the approach to Salonika by the Vardar line portended an aerial attack on a large scale.

The French had reported the arrival of a new scout squadron at Kanatlarci, and information came through from an agent that this squadron had left Leipzig for the Macedonian front at the end of May. In the Monastir region the enemy was so active in the air that it became obvious he was attempting to conceal certain movements which were going on behind his own lines. In this he was unsuccessful. All this activity of the enemy which promised so much faded away without any explanation forthcoming.

On June the 5th, Captain W. D. M. Bell, well known in British East Africa as a big-game hunter, was on escort duty on a B.E.12. Over the Vardar he met a Halberstadt scout fitted with two guns firing forward. He attacked, but after a few rounds his gun jammed and nothing he could do would rectify the stoppage. The German machine broke off the combat, and dived towards Hudova, and Bell returned to Janes. Later in the day it was reported by the French that this machine had been forced to land after the fight, near Mrzenci, a small village about 24 miles north of Guevgueli, and a mile west of the Vardar. Here it was shelled by French naval guns.

The Royal Flying Corps policy of an incessant offensive was fully maintained, but although there were constant bomb-raids, many others that had been planned came to nothing owing to the unusually bad weather. The normal June was a time of oppressive, damp heat in Macedonia. June, 1917, however, proved an exception, and was noted for torrential rain-storms and low clouds, but although the Germans were very active, they never attacked our machines unless we were inferior in numbers. They further at this time did little or no artillery reconnaissance. It has been argued that this was unnecessary owing to excellent observation posts afforded to the enemy by the high ground which he everywhere occupied. The lines had been well sighted and also well prepared, and, whereas they thus dominated our positions, in most cases our Staff were confronted by the problem of what was happening on the other side of the hill. For this reason alone the work of the R.F.C. on this front was of great value.

Six machines of 47 bombed Platanenwald camp on June the 11th. Seven 100-lb. and eighteen 16-lb. bombs were dropped and a good deal of damage done. A little later in the day an unusual incident happened near Rupel. A machine, apparently hostile, but of unknown type, was seen to be approaching Orljak (a 17 Squadron aerodrome) from the direction of Rupel, flying at 6,000 feet. This in itself was unusual, as the enemy seldom crossed the lines under 15,000 feet. Two machines of 17 Squadron went up to attack, but on approaching closely they noticed Allied marking on the wings, and, instead of firing, they forced it to land. The pilot proved to be Staff-Captain Smolianinov, a Russian. He had flown direct from Bolgrad in Roumania, across Bulgaria, in order to join the Allied Forces in Macedonia. He was perturbed at the state of affairs in Russia, and on a captured L.V.G. had decided to join the Allies on the Salonika front in the hope of getting more fighting.

Smolianinov was an interesting character. He held many orders of high distinction. He joined the Russian Artillery in 1909 and learned to fly in 1912. He had flown continuously since the beginning of the war, mostly on captured German machines, which he stated were superior in equipment to anything supplied by the Russians. The L.V.G. on which he made his flight across Bulgaria could not climb above 6,000 feet, and had indeed been in use for more than a year. Permission was given for him to be attached to the R.F.C. as a pilot, and for some time he was with 47 Squadron. Some little time later he returned to Odessa by air.

Just about this time there was a slight withdrawal of our line in the Struma Valley, which is almost uninhabitable in summer owing to the virility of the sand-fly and mosquito. *Struma*, I believe, means "Valley of Death." It was not wrongly named. This move did not affect 47 Squadron, except indirectly, for the Struma Valley was the domain of No. 17.

Among the bomb-raids carried out in the early summer, one of the most successful was on Cerniste dump on June the 21st, when, in addition to five direct hits on sheds and dumps, one bomb fell on a dug-out and completely demolished it. These raids were not seriously interfered with by hostile aircraft, but towards the end of June the enemy became more active. On June the 29th the raiders of 47 were attacked over Bogdanci by three Halberstadts, who were engaged by Denning, Dickson, Brufton, and Gibson. Two of the Halberstadts were driven off and retired towards Hudova, whilst the third, after receiving two drums of ammunition from Lieutenant Gibson at 30 yards' range, went down emitting smoke. It was thought that the machine crashed, although it was not actually seen to do so. In these raids, and on patrols at this time, Pilkington, Scales, Buckingham, Gibson, Croil, Dent, and Wilkinson did particularly good work.

This persistent bombing on our part had very visible effects on the enemy's moral. Fresh antiaircraft guns were constantly being located in new positions. So soon as even a single British aeroplane was sighted, trains moved hurriedly out of stations. In the Angista Valley smoke fires were started at intervals when a reconnaissance machine appeared over Porna. Some of the large dumps were divided up into smaller ones. Others were even moved altogether to Marinopolje, a further 25 miles off, where they were under the dubious protection of new anti-aircraft guns specially and hurriedly brought from Germany.

On July the 5th, Lieutenant R. M. Wynne Eyton on a De Havilland

"The Devil's Eye,"—Bulgarian Observation Post on top of Grand Couronné
(not many got as close as this to it.)

2 was patrolling near Cerniste at about 8,000 feet. He saw, some 200 feet below him, an Albatross two-seater escorted by three Halberstadt scouts. Wynne Eyton singled out the Albatross, which was ranging for the artillery, and dived, firing about 100 rounds at point-blank range. The Albatross dived steeply, emitting smoke, and the 22nd Division later reported that it apparently righted itself just before reaching the ground, but the actual contact with the ground could not be observed. The evidence seems to point to the fact that the Albatross crashed and was destroyed. Wynne Eyton was unable to see what happened, owing to the fact that after sending the Albatross down he climbed to attack the three Halberstadts. These, however, were loath to linger, and made off towards Hudova.

On July the 8th, the squadron suffered a loss in the person of Lieutenant H. C. Brufton. He had engaged an enemy machine according to the following report from the officer commanding No. 24 Anti-Aircraft Section at Bekerli:—

> On July the 8th at 19.30 hours a De Havilland engaged a Halberstadt over Krastali. The De Havilland pilot dived three times to the attack, and on the third occasion he dived very steeply and to great depth. After righting himself he proceeded in the direction of Janes. The Halberstadt took a northerly direction, apparently in great trouble.

Lieutenant Brufton's machine was over the aerodrome at Janes, when it was suddenly seen to break up in the air. Brufton fell out at 3,000 feet and was picked up about 100 yards from the wreckage. Possibly some vital part of the structure had been weakened by hits from explosive bullets, which the German airmen were then using. Lieutenant Brufton was buried in the cemetery near the aerodrome.

During the third week in July there were rumours of serious concentrations behind the enemy lines. No. 47 Squadron were called upon to do an unusually large number of reconnaissances, and as a result of this close watch of the whole enemy area they were able to say that no major movements were going on. This information, which proved to be correct, was most useful to the corps commander. The weather was bad. A turbulent, dusty Vardar wind blew about this time, often accompanied by thick white fogs—a nightmare in the mountainous country. Despite the weather conditions, all the reconnaissances called for by the corps commander were carried out, and the desired information in each case brought back. This reflected great credit on the squadron observers, of whom Lieutenants Boyd-Harvey, Harman, and H. A. Jones were most active. Harman survived many adventures, to succumb to pneumonia at the time of the armistice.

This work called forth the following letter from the XII Corps:—

The corps commander has read the summary of work, carried out by the scouts and patrols under your command yesterday, and is well satisfied with the work carried out during the recent trying weather. He wishes you to inform your flight commanders that he watches their work with interest, and is fully aware of the difficulties with which they have to contend. 20.7.17.

On July the 30th, "A" flight of No. 47 moved from Hadzi-Junas to Kalabac. Kalabac is the name of a bleak, bare peak that rises from the Janes plain. From its summit on a clear day a splendid view is obtainable across Lake Ardzan to the tumbled masses of Lower Serbia; across Lake Doiran to the wall of the Beles Mountains; whilst the hundred square miles of plain show like a carpet intersected by ravines and blotted with poppy patches and ruined villages. At the feet of Kalabac "A" Flight took up their summer abode under the command of Captain W. D. M. Bell, M.C. It was much more bracing than Hadzi-Junas, although not so good an aerodrome.

In the winter an occasional wolf lurked about, but the chief danger in summer came from grass fires which made a rapid way before the wind, and occasionally necessitated whole battalions turning out to combat them. These fires were not confined to Kalabac, but were common throughout Macedonia in summer. Often at night, when some half-dozen were blazing furiously in various directions, an entertaining display was provided if the fires were remote enough to lend the necessary detachment, or else some warm excitement if they were near enough to compel action.

August was hot and sultry. It was weather that made one long for the hills of Scotland or the coast of Cornwall. There was no gratification for these wishes, but August offered many officers of 47 a change of scenery which varied between Turkey and Albania. These were the circumstances. Hostile aircraft operating from Gereviz had caused considerable annoyance by frequent bombing raids on the R.N.A.S. aerodrome at Thasos, and so the R.F.C. were asked to co-operate in two raids on the aerodrome and seaplane base at Gereviz. Only too glad to repay in some measure the invaluable help given them by the R.N.A.S. earlier in the year, the R.F.C. seized this opportunity.

Five machines from 47 were detailed for this work, and they set off for No. 17 aerodrome at Marian. Here they met seven aeroplanes from 17 Squadron, and on August the 10th the formation left Marian for Thasos, which was reached at 7 o'clock after an hour over the land and a second hour over the water. On arrival the machines were ranged round the aerodrome, some in Bessonneaux and some under olive trees.

On the following morning the R.F.C. machines started for Gereviz some 35 to 40 miles away. On this raid 1,410 lb. of bombs were dropped. Three R.N.A.S. machines accompanied the formation: two as bombers, and one, a Sopwith Schneider, as escort. Unfortunately, the Sopwith lagged behind the formation, and three Halberstadts which attacked shot the machine about a good deal, and wounded the pilot in the leg. He was able to return to Thasos, where the wound was found not to be serious. The remainder of the formation were not attacked, probably owing to the very close order kept, and they returned safely at 11 a.m. The machines were at once overhauled and fitted with other bombs for the afternoon raid. Two R.N.A.S. machines accompanied this raid, and 1,964 lb. of bombs were distributed among the hangars on the Gereviz aerodrome.

Once again excellent formation was kept, and the three enemy scouts patrolling over the aerodrome refrained from attacking. All machines were back at Thasos at four o'clock in the afternoon, and after a further overhaul, the last R.F.C. machine had left the ground at 6 p.m. for Salonika, where the formation arrived without mishap. This was a crowded day's work. The results of the two raids may be summarised as follows:—

(1) A petrol or bomb store set on fire and destroyed.

(2) Considerable damage to large seaplane shed containing about three machines.

(3) Damage to a seaplane shed containing probably two machines.

(4) Much damage to camps.

(5) Grass fires started in many places on and about the aerodrome, with consequent probable damage to some of the machines which were near the sheds.

Further co-operation of 47 Squadron during August was with the French near Monastir.

On the evening of August, the 16th a number of aeroplanes of 47 and 17 Squadrons left for a French aerodrome near Florina, for the purpose of carrying out a series of bombing raids in co-operation with the French on hostile camps and aerodromes in this area. The enemy was well equipped and very active in the air.

The British machines were a motley collection. From 47 Squadron there were B.E.12's, Vickers Bullets, and one A.W. fitted with a 140 horsepower R.A.F. engine. This was the only two-seater machine accompanying the detachment, and, with Lieutenant H. J. Scales or Lieutenant F. W. H. Thomas as pilot and Lieutenant H. A. Jones as observer, did some good work. 17 Squadron sent mostly B.E.12's, although three of their pilots were flying Nieuport Scouts which had been obtained from the French. The French were to a certain extent much better equipped, and were well supplied with Spads, Nieuports, and Sopwith 14 strutters. The enemy's best type was the D.V. Albatross.

The programme which had been arranged for the first day was not carried out in full. The French petrol was found not to suit our engines, and there were other difficulties. Further, there were high winds on the succeeding days which sometimes made flying impossible. This is not to say, however, that the enemy did not soon become aware of the arrival of the Flying Corps. On August the 17th and 18th the enemy aerodromes and billets at Kanatlarci were bombed. On the first occasion good results were obtained, but the high wind on the 18th made bombing inaccurate. On August the 19th the dump at Topolcani and buildings at Prilep, which were believed to be occupied by enemy headquarters, were bombed. At the dump a fire was started which burned for forty minutes, and the building believed to be the headquarter offices was destroyed.

The same night Major J. Herring, of No. 17 Squadron, who was commanding the R.F.C. detachment, set out to bomb Prilep. The night was black as velvet, and although Major Herring knew not a yard of the country he picked his way through the valleys and dropped eight bombs on Prilep. Hostile searchlights picked him up over the objective, and he was unable to observe the result of his bombing. He returned safely, and after a short rest was starting on a full day's work on the 20th. Mountainous country offers certain distractions to the night pilot. A French officer who tried a similar feat a day or two later unfortunately collided with a mountain on the return journey and was very seriously injured.

On these various raids hostile opposition was met with. On the morning raid of the 19th, although large numbers of German machines were in the air, few of them attacked with any measure of determination. On this occasion there was a formidable escort of French Spads and Nieuports, and despite the diversities of type, really good formation was kept. Twice, however, German machines got into the very heart of the formation unobtrusively. They shot one or two machines about considerably and eventually succeeded in escaping. They deserved to—the second of the two machines more especially.

This was apparently a two-seater Roland, which opened fire on the leader of the formation from almost point-blank range. It is difficult to say how he got there, but once there, despite a murderous fire from such machines as could open it without fear of hitting a comrade, he hung on tenaciously and came within an ace of bringing the leader down. The observer in the Roland was quickly hit and collapsed over the side of the cockpit. Eventually, however, the enemy machine dived steeply out of the formation, but under complete control. This was a courageous piece of work, and the pilot and observer of the enemy machine earned the admiration of those taking part in the raid, who, despite that they had done their best to shoot them down, were glad they had escaped.

The formation was well kept, despite this attempt and others to break it, and all our machines returned safely.

The raid on Prilep was repeated on the morning of the 20th at the same hour. The aeroplanes left the aerodrome before dawn, before the tops of the mountains were touched by the first rays of the sun, and when mists hung about the valleys. But this time there were mishaps, for, in addition to engine trouble which prevented some of the machines from starting, the French escort never found our small formation. The leader on this occasion was Lieutenant A. Maxwell of No. 17 Squadron, and No. 47 was represented by Lieutenants Scales, Thomas, and H. A. Jones, the former on a B.E.12 and the latter two on the Armstrong-Whitworth. There were three escorting Nieuports. The formation was attacked as soon as the line was reached, and the Nieuports drew off to engage the hostile machines. The remaining three machines flew on and were joined over Prilep by Lieutenants Bamford and Lee of 17 Squadron on Nieuports.

Over the objective, the British machines were fiercely attacked just as the last bombs were released. Lieutenant J. L. Bamford of 17, after a short but gallant fight, went spinning down and was later reported by the enemy to be killed. The leader of the formation which dived on Bamford fell to the observer of the Armstrong-Whitworth, which was now in rear of the other three machines. The enemy formation then turned on to the A.W., and a running fight between the British and German machines ensued, lasting some forty minutes. Lieutenant F. W. H. Thomas, the pilot of the A.W., received a wound in the back as soon as the fight opened, and the observer, Lieutenant H. A. Jones, a hit in the stomach which mostly spent itself on his Sam Browne belt. During the course of the further fighting, Jones received a hit in the mouth, and an explosive bullet in the left hand. Before his Lewis gun was shot out of action, two further enemy machines were sent down, apparently out of control.

Lieutenant Thomas fainted twice in the machine from loss of blood, and the A.W. fell some thousands of feet, but by a superhuman effort Thomas regained control at about 200 feet, many miles behind the enemy's lines, and, encouraged by his observer, succeeded in crossing the trenches at this height despite a heavy fire. He then hung on doggedly and eventually arrived at the aerodrome, where he made a perfect landing. It was his last. His wound, a painful one, which would have crippled him for life had he lived, he bore stoically.

As he fought death in the air, so he fought for life on the ground. But after lingering painfully through 4½ months, during which time he made the journey from Serbia by Salonika and Malta to London, he died of his wounds and was buried in Brookwood cemetery. Thomas, who came from Rhodesia, was a big-game hunter by profession. His death was worthy of his life. (This fight was described in *Blackwood's Magazine*, October, 1918, under the title "A Bombing Stunt—and Afterwards," and is republished at the end of this book.) During this time the squadron at Janes carried on its routine, and a few days after the raid on Prilep described above the machines on detachment at Monastir returned to the squadron.

The hot blaze of summer drew to a close. Everything about the aerodrome looked dry and yellow, patched here and there with black where fire had eaten across the landscape. The waving expanse of asphodel, which had carpeted the foothills near Doiran with a delicate mauve in the early spring, had withered away. The scarlet poppies which had stained the ground throughout the summer drooped and died.

October came round: a mellow month of fine sunsets and perfect nights. In the less fierce blaze of the autumn sun, the men looked bronzed and well, and shook off the torpor of the summer. The squadron did its usual work without any untoward excitement. In October, however, No. 47 suffered some losses. One, 2nd Lieutenant J. R. F. Gubbin, a friend of Thomas, had also come from Rhodesia to join up. Another, Lieutenant E. R. Wilkinson, M.C., was a friend of Bamford, with whom he had shared the adventure in the spring of a collision in the air. The third, 2nd Lieutenant P. D. Montague, was a capable pilot and a charming personality. Wilkinson sustained a fatal wound in the abdomen on October the 6th.

Eight machines had bombed batteries at Nicolic from a low height. From a hundred feet or so on the return journey infantry were attacked with machine-gun fire. Whilst doing this, Wilkinson's machine received a direct hit on the engine by a shell and he was forced to land near Brest. He was further hit in the abdomen, and succumbed to his injuries next day. He had come out with the squadron and did consistently good work over many months.

Gubbin and Montague were killed on October the 29th during an attack on Cestovo Dump—an oft-visited objective. Our machines, which numbered five, were attacked by eight Albatross and Halberstadt scouts, just as our formation broke up for bombing. After a gallant fight, Montague on a single-seater B.E.12 went down in a spin, and Gubbin on an A.W.12, with second Air-Mechanic T. H. Bury as machine-gunner, received a machine-gun burst which practically severed his left arm. Gubbin headed the machine for the British lines, losing height the whole time, but unfortunately, he received a further wound from a piece of anti-aircraft shell in his back.

He then fainted and the machine crashed. He knew no more until he found himself in an enemy hospital with his leg off. He lived on for nearly a fortnight and wrote a letter to his wife, setting forth the particulars of his last flight. This was sent home *via* the Red Cross at Geneva. Gubbin was the son of the late Dr. Brendon Gubbin, of Bristol. He had gone to Rhodesia at the age of seventeen, where he bought a farm. He returned during the war with his wife and small son, and was at once commissioned in the R.F.C. Montague had only one characteristic common to Gubbin and himself, and that was bravery. Otherwise, he was a wholly dissimilar personality. He was tall, good-looking, and had delicate manners. In dress he was untidy as a schoolboy, and when he blushed—as he often did—he looked like one.

His life in Macedonia was one constant enjoyment to himself and an inspiration to those who came in contact with him. He loved flying and was always happy in the air. He was a devoted naturalist, and found so much that was of interest all around him that he was always happy on the ground. If he were wanted, he could usually be found embedded in the thatched roof of some local cottage, only the soles of his boots visible. A tug on the boots and he would emerge, grimy, but grasping a clutch of eggs. But his, and our, great delight was music. He had made in the squadron workshops a lute of quaint design and infinite sweet tone. On this he was wont to beguile the summer nights with medieval ballads, of which he had a representative collection. If, however, the mess was boisterous, Montague's lute played ballads that were not at all medieval.

A month or two later news of Montague came from the enemy in the form of a message written in Bulgarian and dropped on Janes aerodrome by a hostile aeroplane. The translation of the message is as follows:—

On the 29th of October 1917, one of your comrades met with a hero's death in an air fight. He was buried with due honours and a memorial stone has been put up over his grave, but without an inscription, as his name is not known to us. In order that we may make good this deficiency, kindly inform us as to his name and the date and place of his birth. The reply should be addressed 'Bulgarian Airmen.'

On October the 16th, whilst climbing for a raid on the Beles range, one of the machines, with 2nd Lieutenant P. C. Hunter as pilot, and Lieutenant A. S. Butler as observer, stalled at a height of 300 to 400 feet and crashed to the ground near Kirec. The aeroplane caught fire on hitting the ground, and the bombs then exploded, and both officers were killed instantly. They had only joined the squadron a few days before.

These losses, mostly of officers who had been long with the squadron, might easily have had a somewhat depressing effect on its spirit. But the opposite was the case. The example of those who had gone was an inspiration to those who followed on. The tradition of 47 was shaping well.

CHAPTER 8

The Second Winter

The casualties of the autumn were largely due to the enemy's superior machines. The personal prestige set up by our pilots and observers did not always balance against this better equipment. In November, 1917, No. 47 Squadron received a few S.E.5a's. The S.E.5, (*i.e.* the fifth variant of the Scouting Experimental type), a single-seater scout of very high performance, was the most successful machine produced in the war by the Royal Aircraft Factory. It had a fine record in France, and, flown by such officers as Major J. T. B. McCudden, V.C., accounted for a large number of enemy aeroplanes. Its success was no less startling in Macedonia. During the winter, flying weather was bad, so that it was not until the spring and summer of the following year that the full effect of the new machines was apparent. What that effect was will be dealt with in the next chapter.

In addition to the losses caused by enemy activity, malaria and other illnesses had sadly depleted the numbers of the squadron. Reinforcements were asked for from Egypt, and in expectation of these a rearrangement of the flights took place. "A" Flight moved from Kalabac to Hadzi-Junas for the winter, "B" Flight and Headquarters remained at Janes, and "C" Flight at Kirec. At this time "A" Flight was a scout flight, whilst "B" and "C" shared the rest of the work between them. This was not altogether satisfactory. Owing to the great variety of work undertaken and the large area over which the flights had to operate, it was difficult for a pilot or observer to get thoroughly acquainted with any particular area.

Valuable time was sometimes lost by "C" Flight receiving its orders second-hand through the squadron office at Janes. For these reasons, and in order that pilots and observers should keep in closer touch with the artillery, it was decided to separate "B" and "C" Flights, and "C" Flight at Kirec was to do nothing but artillery work, whilst "B" Flight at Janes was to do the rest of the work required for the XII Corps.

Lieutenant J. C. O. Dickson was taken from "A" Flight and given command of "C" Flight at Kirec, and Captain MacDonald, the artillery liaison officer, was moved from Janes and attached to "C" Flight, which now came directly under the orders of the artillery command of the XII Corps. The flight worked under the counter-battery staff officer, Lieutenant-Colonel Crawford.

Captain Dickson says:

The new arrangement, proved most satisfactory. It was now possible to keep in very close touch with the Corps artillery staff, the members of which seemed to take a personal interest in every pilot and observer in the flight. A special effort was also made to make battery commanders, and the officers in the flight working with them, personally acquainted. Gunner officers were enticed to the Mess at Kirec, and there were meetings of both parties at the Heavy Artillery Headquarters. By discussions, before and after shoots, misunderstandings were reduced to a minimum, and shoots were carried out extraordinarily smoothly and rapidly.

The battery commanders, always kind and considerate, spared no efforts to assist pilots and observers, both by means of information on the ground, and when in the air, in the hundred and one ways in which they could do so.

The map difficulty still gave rise to trouble. "C" Flight, by reason of their work, probably came up against this difficulty most. All the maps, with the exception of the small-scale German ones, had been compiled entirely from aerial photos, without any possible chance of making corrections by means of ground observations. It was found impossible, in many areas, to locate a point on the ground by means of the maps supplied. This was rather disconcerting for new arrivals in the squadron. The errors in the maps were forcibly demonstrated by a somewhat heated discussion which took place after a series of destructive shoots.

The gunners and sound-rangers produced calculations which seemed to prove that the shots had fallen 300 or 400 yards from the various targets, while "C" Flight retaliated by showing photographs of the positions, taken before and after the shoots, proving that the fire had been very effective. The survey section was called in to arbitrate, and found that the whole of the north-western shore of Lake Doiran was marked, on existing maps, about a quarter of a mile from its proper position, and that the surrounding country was correspondingly wrong. This map difficulty was got over to some extent by using squared photographs.

About this time the photography on the front began to receive more attention. "C" Flight carried out experiments on stereoscopic photography with such success that "the Corps Artillery Staff," says Captain Dickson, "refused to take more than a polite interest in any photos that were not stereoscopic." Very large areas were taken, so that stereo-prints could be made of any suspicious points in the area. These areas finally included the whole front from Lake Doiran to the Vardar.

Rapid results were made possible by attaching a small photographic section of five N.C.O.'s and men to the flight. This section developed all negatives and made two prints of each, the plates being then sent to the main section at the base, where any further copies asked for were produced. The work of this small section was extraordinary, a print of every plate exposed during the day being ready by six o'clock to be taken to Corps Artillery Headquarters.

Bombing raids were made now in great force, and all available machines were used, not only from both 17 and 47 Squadrons, but also from the French aviation service. The enemy aerodrome at Hudova on the banks of the silver winding Vardar; the large enemy dumps at Cerniste and Cestovo, which lay in the valley beyond the maze of the Grand Couronné hills; the enemy headquarters at Platanenwald in the flatter country near Bogdanci; Furka, and many other places, were constantly raided. The Bulgar must have had a very annoying time throughout these days. He was repeatedly hit, whilst his seconds were so busily occupied elsewhere as to preclude their offering him anything more satisfactory than a chastened moral support.

On November the 14th, whilst engaged on a photographic reconnaissance, 2nd Lieutenant E. Brewer was attacked by an enemy scout and received a bullet in the neck. Both his petrol tanks were shot through, but he was able to make a forced landing near Corsica behind our lines. In his laboured descent he flew perilously low over a certain headquarters and a little later on, the brigadier commanding, ignorant of course of the reason for this, had some pointed remarks to make on the futility of dangerous low stunting by the pilots of the Flying Corps. The Macedonian climate was trying.

On November the 21st, machines of 47, combined with others of 17 Squadron, raided a divisional headquarters at a small town called Vesnik, east of Seres. Seres is a comparatively important town at the foot of the hills, where they merge into the Struma plain. It is situated on the Salonika-Constantinople railway, and gave its name to the road which goes to it from Salonika. The Seres road was the main artery of the Struma front, and was the more important because of the absence of railway communication. This weary, congested road was dust-laden in summer and sometimes wellnigh impassable in winter.

An event which happened on November the 21st comes outside the history of 47 Squadron, except in so far as the victim of the exploit had often fought the machines of the squadron. This was the death of Ober-Leutnant von Eschwege, a gallant German aviator who was well known to the Royal Flying Corps on this front. The balloon of No. 17 Section had been repeatedly and successfully attacked, and an anti-aircraft device was fixed to an old balloon. On November the 21st the balloon, without observer, was attacked at close range. The device was successful and the hostile machine broke up in the air, and the pilot who was killed was identified, from documents found on the body, as von Eschwege.

A message was dropped over the enemy lines giving information of the death of this pilot, and on the following day a German machine came over Monhui and dropped a wreath, a flag, and a letter addressed to the Royal Flying Corps Marian (No. 17 Squadron). Part of the message was as follows:—

We thank you sincerely for your information regarding our comrade Lieut. von Eschwege and request you to permit the accompanying wreath and flag to be placed on his last resting-place.

Deutsches Fliegerkommando.

This was done. The Bulgarian Official Communiqué of the same day contained the following:—

The German Lieutenant von Eschwege, who today obtained his twentieth victory in the air, was brought down by enemy anti-aircraft fire and found, in the air, a glorious death. The Bulgarian army, which has always valued highly the brave deeds of this rare and courageous aviator, will hold his name in living and unforgetful memory.

Towards the end of the year there was a good deal of night bombing. At 10 p.m. on November the 28th four enemy machines dropped sixteen high-explosive bombs and several incendiary bombs on Janes

The Death of Von Eschwege

aerodrome. The aiming was good. Four mechanics were wounded and a bell tent burned, but no other damage done. Reprisals were made in kind, and night after night, at repeated intervals, the enemy aerodromes and dumps were raided by us. This night bombing had the effect of spreading the activity over the twenty-four hours.

On the morning of the raid on Janes aerodrome Lieutenant B. R. Apps and Lieutenant A. S. Clark, observer, on an A.W.12, were taking photographs over Bogorodica. They were attacked by two enemy scouts, one of which was sent down out of control, and the other, after receiving several bursts from the observer's gun at 50 yards' range, gave up the uneven combat. In the afternoon, 2nd Lieutenant J. C. Nelson, with Lieutenant A. J. Pick, observer, went out to photograph the machine which had been sent down out of control by Apps and Clark in the morning. When passing over Stojakovo, the British two-seater and a B.E.12 on which was 2nd Lieutenant F. Henwood were attacked by three enemy scouts. Both the machines of No. 47 fired off all their ammunition from close range, and one of the enemy machines crashed into the hills north of Bogdanci. This machine was later photographed.

On the last day of the month, Captain R. M. Wynne Eyton, with 2nd Lieutenant W. D. Robertson, observer, fought for a long time with an enemy aeroplane. It was a long, indecisive duel, and both the officers of 47 were wounded, but landed safely.

On December the 19th, 2nd Lieutenant F. D. Travers, who was escorting a photographing machine on a B.E.12, was attacked by a D.III Albatross scout. He obtained a position above the enemy, and then dived, opening fire with three Lewis guns. His tracer ammunition was seen to be sparkling into and around the enemy machine, which went down in a spin for several thousand feet until it was lost sight of by Travers. Anti-aircraft sections reported seeing this machine go down out of control, but it was not possible to see it crash owing to intervening hills.

The weather in December was severe. The usual Vardar winds, accompanied by snow and rain, made living uncomfortable, and, on at least twelve days during the month, flying impossible. If, however, it was at all possible to get a machine into the air, the work required by the XII Corps artillery was attempted. These attempts were much appreciated by the corps commander, as will be seen from this letter, received by the general officer commanding the Royal Artillery:—

The corps commander has instructed me to express through you, to the batteries and R.F.C. observers concerned, his appreciation of the good work done during the past month in destructive shoots.

Batteries 13th, 18th, 186th, 190th, and 201st Heavies, and 43rd, 130th, 138th Siege.

Observers and pilots, 2/Lieuts. Taylor, Rose, Collier, Brandt, and Lieuts. Leaver and Dickson.

The first day of January for No. 47 Squadron, as for all other units on the fighting fronts, came along very much like all the other days that had preceded it. The first casualties of the year occurred on the third day of the month. Three Armstrong-Whitworths on photographic duty were attacked by three enemy scouts near Cestovo. After a short combat one of the A.W.'s, with 2nd Lieutenant H. A. Tracey, pilot, and Lieutenant A. Rowan, observer, went down in a spin, but afterwards flattened out and was seen to land north of Lake Doiran. Shortly afterwards clouds of smoke were observed to come from the machine, "and," says the official record, 'it was believed that the occupants landed safely and then destroyed the machine." A little further light was thrown on to the fate of these two officers by the enemy wireless two days later, it stated:

An English aeroplane was brought down by a German sergeant-major in an air combat, and fell behind our lines northwest of Lake Doiran. The occupants, two Englishmen, were made prisoners.

What actually happened is told by Tracey in his own words:—

I noticed three enemy aircraft approaching from Cestovo. ... Before we closed, one of the enemy dived towards Hudova, and then the remaining two opened out on to the machines in front of me. Then—exactly how it got there I never knew—one of their machines started to fire into me from the tail, and then R.'s gun jammed, and at the same time the engine petered out. This was over Furka, and I found that with luck I should be able to get to the lines; but as the bullets were passing through my legs I decided to spin out of reach. When I came out the Hun recommenced to shoot, so I had to spin again, and when I got into flying position once more the lines were out of gliding distance, and I had to land on the level piece of ground at the foot of the Grand Couronné.

The first arrival was a Bulgar who had a double-barrelled shotgun and who galloped round us on a pony shouting something that neither Rowan nor I could understand. Shortly afterwards several more Bulgar soldiers came up, as well as one or two German Tommies, and we were then in a nasty ring of the enemy. At last, they noticed that the machine was on fire (we had fired a Very's light into the cockpit where the petrol had collected from the tank, which was riddled).

We were then taken to a dug-out at the back of Grand Couronné. This was the headquarters of a battery of small howitzers. Here they took away all that we possessed and only gave us back our cigarettes, keeping all our money and our caps and gloves.

After a meal of rice and skilly we were marched towards Furka, and about half-way there we got a conveyance to the divisional headquarters. Here the Hun flying corps took charge of us, and we were given some chocolate and coffee before being motored to Hudova.

We were kept at Hudova for two or three days, and all the time we were well supplied with drinks to try to get us to give away information whilst in an inebriated state.

On the night of January 5/6, we were taken to Uskub by train and put into the local gaol. Then the Hun wing headquarters sent for us and gave us some breakfast about 12.30. After a second examination we were sent on. The train was nearly the death of both of us, as there was no way to keep warm, and by the time we got to Nish, we were far from feeling anything, and it was all we could do to change into the Sofia train. At 6.0 a.m. in the morning of the 7th of January, we reached Sofia, and three more hours in a local train brought us to Kjustendil. Here we were marched to the War Office, and had our first meal since we left Hudova (the breakfast at Uskub was only a couple of sandwiches).

The rest of the day was taken up in final cross-examination, but I do not think they got anything out of us, as we were too fed up with the people and their customs to give them anything less than poison.

In the evening we set out again for Sofia, where we spent the night. On the following day we got to the prisoners-of-war camp at Philippopolis.

Of our life at the camp there is not too much to say that has not been put into print already. The barrack that was allotted to British officers had been used as a cholera hospital prior to the war. The floor was stone and the walls were made of wattle and daub, which in many cases allowed the frogs to come into the building. As all the windows were warped the snow used to pour in. When it rained, the roof dripped water in such quantities that we could not keep dry.

The furniture per officer was a bedstead, two very thin blankets, and a palliasse which we were expected to fill with straw. The food for the 36-42 officers was not sufficient to feed two healthy men.

Once a week we were allowed to go to the Turkish bath.

Of all the attempts to escape there was not one which was successful, though some of the officers made a very good try and managed to get as far as the coast, where they signalled one of our patrol boats. They were recaptured before they had time to inform the patrol boat of their identity."

This narrative, which gives a picture of the life that awaited the unfortunate people who were forced to come down behind the enemy lines, has carried us ahead of the story.

At 4.30 in the afternoon of January the 18th, 2nd Lieutenant P. A. Boss, on a B.H.12, set out with six 20-lb. and two incendiary bombs to attack the Bulgarian Headquarters at Kjustendil, some 90 miles from the aerodrome. He was timed to reach the objective just before dark, but owing to strong unexpected winds encountered during the outward flight of 24 hours, he arrived late, and in the darkness saw his bombs burst in the centre of the town, but was unable to observe their effect. Boss returned to the aerodrome at 8.15.

During January the S.E.5's and Sopwith Camels and Bristol Monoplanes were taken into use by both 47 and 17 Squadrons.

On January the 24th, two enemy scouts attacked a reconnaissance machine and escorts. One of our machines, piloted by 2nd Lieutenant J. Boyd, with 2nd Lieutenant J. S. Jones as observer, engaged one of the enemy from close range. This apparently went down out of control. The other scout was successfully driven off. An observation post in the line subsequently reported having seen one enemy machine come down in flames after a short combat with one of our aeroplanes, and a second machine was seen to go down out of control. This statement was also confirmed by the intelligence officer of the 66th Infantry Brigade of the 22nd Division.

The next variation in the work came as a result of the attempt by the *Goeben* and *Breslau* to make a sortie from the Dardanelles. These two German cruisers had had an adventurous career. On the outbreak of war, they were in the Mediterranean, and after bombarding the Algerian coast, they eluded the British battleships waiting for them and eventually reached Constantinople. There they were ostensibly sold to the Turkish Government and were renamed.

According to the evidence of German officers, the sortie of these two vessels on January 20th, 1918, had a twofold object: (*a*) to destroy the British monitors and other craft watching the entrance of the Dardanelles, and to do as much damage as possible to the naval base at Mudros; (*b*) to raise the moral of the navy, especially of the German crews. The adventure was made possible by the fact that the Russian naval power in the Black Sea had been withdrawn, as a result of which sufficient coal had become available for large naval operations. Up to this time, the destruction of the Zagouldac coalfields by Russian warships had seriously affected the coal supply of Turkey and of Constantinople in particular. Furthermore, the Turkish authorities had heard that the British submarine which had constantly been in Kephalo Bay had been withdrawn, and it was considered that in consequence a sortie could be made with little risk.

Accordingly in the early morning of January the 20th these two cruisers, accompanied by four Turkish torpedo-boat destroyers, proceeded through the Dardanelles, passing Nagara Net at about 4 a.m. and Seddel Bahr at 5 a.m. The location of the British mines was known to the enemy commanders, partly as a result of extensive aerial reconnaissances. The plans for the sortie allowed for the *Goeben* sailing right over the mines, as it was calculated that owing to her special construction a mine could not do much damage. Actually, she struck a mine when steaming to the westward of Mavro, but this was not allowed to affect the programme.

At 8a.m., with *Breslau* two miles ahead, fire was opened by both ships on to monitors and patrol boats in Kusu Bay. The monitors were sunk. Meantime the four Turkish destroyers, owing to their inferior speed, were left waiting off the entrance to the Dardanelles.

Mudros was the next objective, and course was altered southwards. Soon after turning, the *Breslau* was attacked by a Royal Naval Air Ser-

On board the Goeben after the Armistice

General Coby   Rear–Admiral Arif–Pasha   Captain Stavely, R.N.

vice machine on which the anti-aircraft guns of the *Goeben* opened fire. The shells from the *Goeben* began to fall about the *Breslau*, and so the latter was ordered to take station ahead. In overhauling *Goeben*, *Breslau* struck a mine which blew off both screws and rudder and the stern of the ship. It was soon apparent that *Breslau* could not float, and so *Goeben* proceeded alone to finish the programme. Shortly afterwards the *Breslau* struck three more mines and sank. About 9 a.m., when steering south-south-westward towards Mudros, *Goeben* struck a second mine, as a result of which the admiral decided to abandon the attack on Mudros and return to Constantinople. On the way back, harassed all the while by naval aircraft, the *Goeben* had difficulty in picking her way. Before passing Seddel Bahr at about 11 a.m. she had struck a third mine.

Off Nagara Point there was a misunderstanding about the position of the buoys, and at 12.30 p.m. *Goeben* ran aground. Here, from the afternoon of the 20th until the afternoon of the 26th, the *Goeben* lay at the mercy of air attacks. On the 26th, the salvage operations which had been going forward all the time ended successfully and *Goeben* was towed off and proceeded to Constantinople under her own steam. Here she arrived on the morning of the 27th—the *Kaiser's* birthday. There was no outward manifestation of a happier moral to compensate the crew of the *Goeben* on her arrival.

The *Goeben*, then, escaped. A full account of the aircraft operations whilst the battle cruiser was aground is outside the scope of this narrative, but one or two facts will be stated in passing. The main work fell on the Royal Naval Air Service stationed in these waters, and the help given by the R.F.C. was small. That help was called for on the 21st of January, and, acting under instructions from Sir George Milne, 16th Wing agreed to send six bombing machines at once. Within two hours the first three from No. 17 Squadron left Salonika. The three machines from No. 47 did not arrive at the base in time to go forward that night. They flew to Mudros on the morning of the following day, January the 22nd. They were B.E.12's, piloted by Captain W. R. B. McBain, 2nd Lieutenant P. A. Boss, and 2nd Lieutenant J. A. Beeney. Some 10,000 gallons of aviation spirit were also sent by destroyer.

The following day a further request was received by telegram from "Britannia, Mudros" for another flight of bombers complete with fighters and mechanics. To this G.H.Q. replied, on Wing advice, that four bombers could be sent, but no fighters. Accordingly on January the 25th three B.E.12's and one A.W., piloted by 2nd Lieutenants

Henwood and Dickson and Sergeants Spargo and Dowsett, were despatched. The first two arrived safely. Spargo landed owing to engine trouble at Iviron on Athos Peninsula. Dowsett got lost and finished at Stavros. Other machines were not sent until the 28th owing to stormy weather intervening. Then it was too late.

On their arrival on January the 22nd the R.F.C. machines made ready for a raid, and on that and the two succeeding days the machines made constant day and night attacks on the Goeben. On the 25th the weather became very squally, with low clouds over the Peninsula, and although the R.F.C. machines attempted a raid, they made little headway against the weather and the raid proved abortive. Heavy anti-aircraft fire was met with on all these raids. The Royal Naval Air Service were meantime giving the *Goeben* little rest. Altogether some 270 flights were made and 15 tons of bombs were dropped. Only one bomb of all these seems to have hit the cruiser, and this did a little damage to a funnel. This result was achieved not without losses.

The *Goeben* was, when aground, well protected by anti-aircraft guns and aeroplanes and seaplanes which made correct aiming difficult. The weather was not propitious for aircraft operations. Chiefly, however, the bombs seem to have been far too small in weight in attacking ships. Those used were the only ones available, and were of 65 lb. or 112 lb. weight.

One Turkish officer who took part in these operations stated that at first the crew were very perturbed by our raiding aircraft, and all hands took cover. When they saw the poor results of our first attempts, however, they were encouraged, and for the later attempts, on the approach of our aircraft, boats were immediately manned *to collect the fish*.

In February the Macedonian winter set in. On the night of the 16-17th there was a heavy fall of snow which impeded traffic, broke down telephonic communication between the fronts, and stopped flying for three days. The fall of snow caused a *bessonneau* hangar at Hadzi-Junas aerodrome to collapse, and two B.E.12's and one Vickers Bullet were completely destroyed, and two Vickers Bullets, one S.E.5a, and one Bristol monoplane were damaged. After the snowstorm abated, the sun quickly melted the snow off the plains, but the enemy positions, because they were situated at a higher altitude, remained covered, and thus we were able to take some tale-telling photographs of the enemy trenches and gun-positions.

On March the 13th, Major F. F. Minchin handed over the command of No. 47 Squadron to Major G. D. Gardner, M.C. Major

HOW OCCUPIED TRENCHES SHOW UP IN SNOW

Minchin returned to England.

On April the 1st, 1918, the Royal Air Force came into being, and on that day, in accordance with Air Ministry instructions, No. 150 Squadron was formed in Macedonia as a fighting squadron. On the 26th of April, "A" Flight of No. 17 Squadron became "A" Flight of No. 150 Squadron at Marian under the command of Captain G. E. Gibbs, M.C. "A" Flight of No. 47 Squadron became "B" Flight of No. 150 at Kirec under the command of Captain A. G. Goulding, M.C. "C" Flight was formed at Kirec under Captain H. J. Scales, M.C., at the beginning of May. No. 150 was commanded by Major W. R. B. McBain, who had been with 47 for a considerable time.

So far as those members of the squadron are concerned, the history is ended. They had been with 47 for many months, and many of the mechanics had come out from Beverley with the original squadron. No. 150 Squadron did much to drive the Germans out of the air on the Macedonian front. They carried out well over 2,000 patrols and escorts, destroyed thirty-four enemy machines, and captured two others, whilst they lost only one machine over the enemy lines. Captain H. J. Scales was killed as a result of a flying accident in June, 1918. His loss was keenly felt by all those in 47 who had flown with him. Tall, always immaculate, generous to a degree, and a keen flier who sought the most dangerous jobs, Captain Scales was a loss to the Air Force.

HOW A BATTERY SHOWS UP IN EHE SNOW

CHAPTER 9

The Final Push

On June the 19th, Lieut.-Colonel G. E. Todd took over command of the 16th Wing from Lieut.-Colonel G. W. P. Dawes, when the latter went to England.

During the summer of 1918 formations made up of aeroplanes from 47, 17, and 150 Squadrons constantly raided enemy dumps, and also combined with machines from Stavros in a raid on Drama aerodrome.

On June the 24th, an Armstrong-Whitworth of 47, with Lieutenant D. L. Graham as pilot and Lieutenant A. G. Kane as observer, was observing for the artillery on to an enemy battery. The machine was hit by an anti-aircraft shell and came down in flames. A few weeks later there were further casualties from the same cause. On the morning of July, the 17th, No. 17 Squadron raided Hudova and lost an Armstrong-Whitworth and two officers shot down in flames by anti-aircraft fire. When they heard the news, No. 47 raided Hudova, doing considerable damage, and received from Sir George Milne the following telegram:—

I congratulate the Royal Air Force on its successful raids on Hudova aerodrome this morning, and particularly on the spirit which prompted the second raid. . . .

Another victim of anti-aircraft fire was Captain C. H. Taylor of 47, who was carrying out a photographic reconnaissance of the Vardar Valley on July the 26th. He was a long way over the lines when he was badly hit in the arm by a piece of shell. He was able to return safely.

Major F. A. Bates, M.C., took over command of 47 Squadron on August the 1st from Captain B. E. Berrington, who had been acting for Major G. D. Gardner, M.C. Major Gardner was invalided to England. Major Bates thus commanded the squadron during the period of its greatest activity. That the squadron was completely ready for the heavy work which it was soon called upon to do, is due, not a little, to his great organising ability.

From prisoners taken during the month of June the fact of a lowering of moral in the Bulgarian Army was learnt. It seemed that the Bulgarian Higher Command meditated an attack on the Allies on a large scale from the Doiran front to the sea. Many enemy units, however, were in a state bordering on mutiny and refused to obey orders. Meantime, dramatic changes in the whole situation were preparing. On June the 8th, 1918, General Guillaumat, who had taken over command of the Allied Armies from General Sarrail in December, 1917, was transferred to an important appointment in France. He was succeeded at Salonika by General Franchet d'Esperey, with whose name the brilliant events that were to follow so quickly will always be associated.

The general offensive of the Allied Armies was timed to take place during the first fortnight in September. The British were to take the heights to the west and north-east of Lake Doiran. Preparations went on throughout August. Infantry battalions were gradually withdrawn from the line and carefully trained for the coming attack.

This month of preparation proved a strenuous period for 47 Squadron, and it may be of interest to describe briefly the varied work of each flight.

A new "A" Flight, under Captain J. R. Milne, D.F.C., was formed to replace the flight transferred to 150 Squadron in April, 1918. It was equipped with a type of two-seater aeroplane new to the British Salonika Force—De Havilland 9 (designed by Mr. Geoffrey de Havilland), with 230 H.P. Siddeley Puma engine—the first machine being received in the squadron on August the 2nd. It says much for the work of this newly formed flight that between September the 1st and 29th the flying time of this D.H.9 Flight was 315½ hours. Their work was for the most part long army reconnaissance, and just before armistice hour on 30th September two of their machines penetrated to Sofia, taking photographs and reporting on the progress of the Bulgar rout.

"'B" Flight had the special task during August of photographing back areas of enemy country between the Vardar and the Beles mountains as far as Strumica to form a mosaic map covering upwards of 350 square miles. This was successfully carried out and a mosaic map of the country was printed by the wing photographic section in time for distribution to the corps before the attack. This flight also obtained a series of oblique photos of the enemy front lines taken from an altitude of a few hundred feet, which were of great value to the infantry. In addition, training was carried out in contact patrol practice, using Klaxon horns and signalling panels, with different infantry brigades of XII Corps in turn.

On "C" Flight, under Captain H. G. Davis, D.F.C., devolved primarily the duties of co-operation with the artillery. Daily this flight was occupied from morning till night with counter-battery work—wire-cutting—photographing the enemy lines and gun-positions, etc. The illustration of Guevgueli Bridge after bombardment, with aerial observation, is a good example of their work.

It was clear from air observers' reports that the enemy knew an attack was impending. His reserves were reported in the Vardar Valley, and, to prevent their withdrawal, operations were begun on September the 1st on the right bank of the Vardar against the rocky and heavily fortified salient north of Alcah Makale. These operations were successful, but were only preliminary to the main attack.

On September the 14th the general attack began. Along the diversified line stretching for 80 miles from Lake Doiran to Monastir there was an intense bombardment. Twenty-four hours after the attack opened, Franco-Serbian troops stormed the Bulgar trenches on the mountain heights from Sokol to Vetrenik. By noon the enemy's first and second lines were taken and the way opened for an advance to the heights of Kozyak.

The British were to make their attack only if the Franco-Serbian troops pierced the enemy's line. This condition was now fulfilled, and the morning of September the 18th was fixed for the British effort. The scene of the attack was the ground which held so many memories of the failures of the spring of 1917—the "P" Ridge and the neighbouring heights. Ancillary to the main attack, an attack was to be made round the east and north sides of the lake. The British, for these difficult operations, were, as a result of a sudden and devastating attack of influenza, down to below one-half their normal establishment. Sir George Milne consequently received reinforcements of Greek and French troops.

From the 14th to the 18th of September there was a fierce bombardment. This was intensified before dawn on September the 18th, when the attack was launched. The spring attack of the previous year had been costly. By September, 1918, the Bulgar had many more concrete machine-gun emplacements, and for some eighteen months had been engaged in strengthening his already strong positions. It was de-

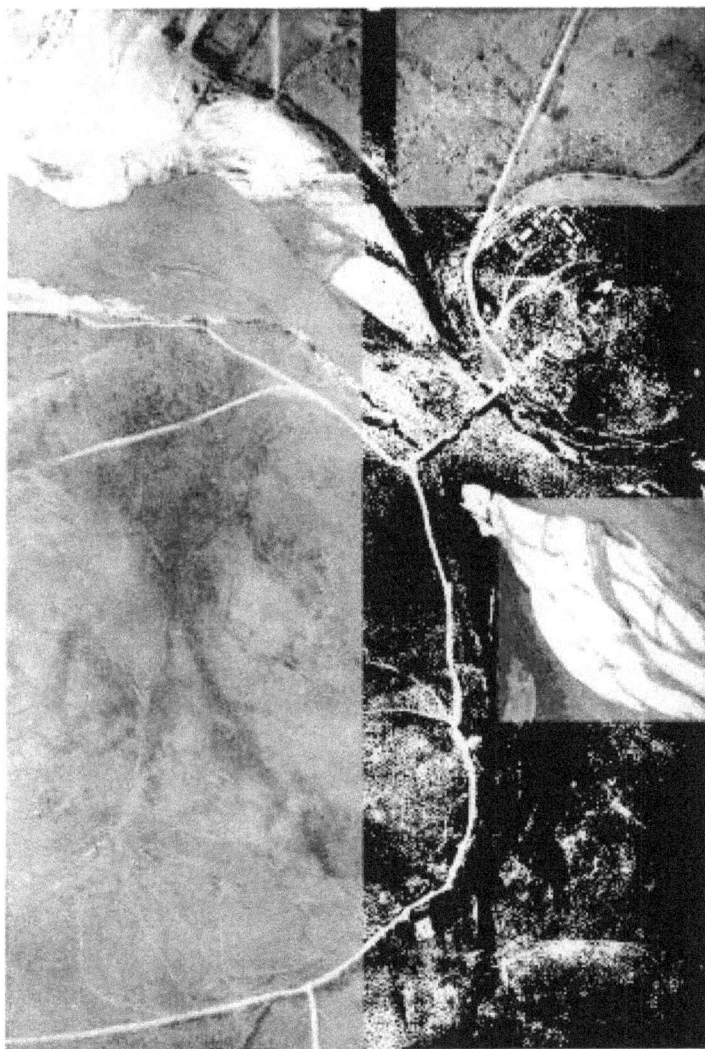

GUEVGUELI BRIDGE ON SEPTEMBER 3RD, 1918—AFTER BOMBARDMENT

cided that zero hour—the hour for launching the attack—would be 105 minutes before sunrise, that is at 05.08 a.m. on the morning of the 18th. All concerned were notified by a code telephone message which was as flippant as the meaning was grave. It ran:—

"508 bottles of beer will be sent to you."

Of the attack itself there is little to say here. The troops advancing against the "P" Ridge persevered with skill and self-sacrifice, but were compelled to fall back, losing three men out of every five. The troops nearer the lake had pushed their attack to the very foot of the Grand Couronné. Chiefly, however, owing to the failure on the "P" Ridge, they too had to fall back. Their loss is perhaps best summarized in one fact, that, of the whole battalion of the 7th Battalion South Wales Borderers, 19 unwounded men and 1 wounded officer survived. It was imperative, however, that the enemy reserves be pinned down to this sector, and a renewal of the attack was ordered for the following day. During the night of the 18th/19th a heavy bombardment was maintained. At 5 a.m. on the morning of the 19th, Greek and Scottish troops moved forward against the lower slopes of the Grand Couronné.

Once again, despite the heavy machine-gun fire, they succeeded in reaching their objective at many points. Several of the intermediate works were captured and held against determined counter-attacks. On the Allied left, French troops, who were assembling in Doldzeli wood, were caught in a heavy barrage and could make no further progress. In spite of this the 65th Infantry Brigade, which had moved up rapidly during the night from an influenza camp, twice tried to capture the "P" Ridge, but were driven back with great losses. Consequently, the troops in the centre had their flanks exposed and fell back, losing heavily. Orders were issued for the ground won to be consolidated, and no further attacks were made. The ground won included Petit Couronne, Teton Hill, and Doiran Town.

Measured in square miles, this was little for the life that had been poured out, but the chief result of the attacks was that the enemy was pinned down to the Vardar front and severely handled at a time when the Franco-Serbian troops were pushing rapidly forward to turn the Bulgarian front and cut its communications. By the morning of the 21st the Franco-Serbian Army had reached the line Gradista-Bosava-Dragosil, and the battle was virtually won. By noon on the 21st it became clear that the enemy was preparing for a hurried retreat from the Doiran Front. During this retreat the work of the Royal Air Force was a dominant factor, and it is here that we must go back to them and tell of their doings in these movements.

No. 47 was disposed for the attack as follows:—

"C" Flight with a strength of seven machines was stationed at Janes and used for artillery work.

"B" Flight with a strength of four machines was at Hajdarli for contact patrols and corps reconnaissance. (Two of these machines, fitted with wireless, were to reinforce the artillery co-operation machines.)

"A" Flight, stationed at Hajdarli with seven machines, was at the disposal of the army for bombing, machine-gunning, and reconnaissance of back areas. One of these machines was fitted with long-distance wireless to communicate direct with corps headquarters.

During the battle the artillery machines did great service. The observers knew the ground by heart and were experienced in observing over the area. Consequently, their work was most efficient. In addition, the enemy was bombed and attacked by machine-gun fire from low heights.

The gunners were appreciative of the work done for them by 47. The B.G. Royal Artillery at XII Corps wrote to Colonel Todd enclosing the following note from Lieut.-Colonel Crawford:—

I would like to bring to notice the excellent work performed by the 47th Squadron R.A.F. in assisting counterbattery work during the operations of the 18th and 19th.
On September the 18th there were 151 N.F. calls.
On September the 19th there were 121 N.F. calls.
"These large numbers speak for themselves and reflect the ighest credit on the observers.

In his covering note, General Holbrooke. said:—

I should like to say how grateful we gunners are for the exceedingly fine work of 47 Squadron during the late battle.
As Colonel Crawford points out, the above figures speak for themselves. Owing to the smoke and dust kicked up by the bombardment and barrage, it was only possible for the large numbers of N.F. calls to be observed by aeroplanes vertically above the target at a low altitude."

The contact patrols were carried out from an exceedingly low height, machines coming down to 200 and 300 feet, which meant that they were often well below the hill-tops and in the thick of the barrage. But the work was done, and messages were dropped on brigade and divisional headquarters, giving the progress in the attacks of the advancing infantry. One of these contact machines received a direct hit and came down in flames. The pilot, Lieutenant J. A. Brandt, and the observer, 2nd Lieutenant H. Gerhardi, were killed. During the advance on the following day the bodies of these officers were found and buried by the British infantry.

Lieutenant Brandt joined the Royal Flying Corps as a mechanic in January, 1915. In June, 1917, he was recommended for a commission and joined a school of aeronautics in Egypt. He graduated in September, 1917, and was posted to Salonika. In July, 1918, he was given leave and came to England. The news of the events pending in the Near East reached him, and he impressed the Air Ministry with his anxiety to return and was allowed to do so before his leave was up. He arrived just in time for the attack. Lieutenant Gerhardi was born in Cape Colony. He joined up at once on the outbreak of war and went through the campaigns in German South-West and German East Africa.

During the battle, opportunity of special adventure was offered to volunteers from 47 and 17 Squadrons. Two were called for to undertake the landing of two British infantry officers behind the enemy's line. The arrangement was that if the landing were successful the machines should return later and pick up the officers again. Lieutenant W. J. Buchanan and Lieutenant J. Boyd volunteered from 17 and 47 respectively.

This is Boyd's report dated 19th September, 1918.—Machine B.E.2e.—Pilot, Lieutenant James Boyd.—Passenger, Lieutenant Lamb, Royal Scots Fusiliers.

> I left Janes aerodrome at 16.55 hours and met escorts as arranged over Kukus at 17.45 hours at 9,000 feet.
>
> At 18.48 I landed about 5 miles north of Strumica; close to the river Stara. Lieut. Lamb at once got out with his kit. I took off within half a minute of landing and Lieut. Lamb made off towards a clump of trees and bushes on the banks of the Stara River, 100 yards away. Lieut. Lamb seemed to know his position and was confident of getting away unseen. When gliding down I pointed out to him the town of Strumica.
>
> Before landing, I flew low over the ground to make sure no one was near. I only observed one man, and he was a peasant riding

a mule. He was over a mile from where I landed and was going in the opposite direction. I flew over him at 200 feet, but beyond turning his head he took no interest in my movements. The nearest village was over 2 miles away and I observed no movements in it. Ten minutes after landing, the valley was in darkness. I am confident Lieut. Lamb escaped unseen. The peasant could not be seen from the landing-ground. I landed in a field of stubble, the surface of which, for at least 200 yards square, was fairly good.

On 'taking off' I rejoined the escort and returned to Hajdarli aerodrome at 19.30 hours.

Lieutenant Buchanan was less fortunate. He did not return. The escort from 47 Squadron who accompanied him made the following report on their return:—

We beg to report that on the 19th we were detailed as escort to Lieut. Buchanan on a special mission. Together with Captain Edwards and two S.E.5a's we left the rendezvous at 17.45 hours, climbing, and crossed the Beles mountains north of Poroj at 11,500 feet. As soon as we had crossed the Beles, Lieut. Buchanan glided rapidly downwards in the direction of Petric. We followed to 2,500 feet (aerodrome height), when, owing to dust and the wooded nature of the ground, we lost sight of his machine just about the junction of the Strumica and Mendova Rivers. At 18.45 hours approximately we again picked up his machine climbing just about this point. He had then been lost to us for approximately two minutes. He flew west for a short time, then turned round and went towards the northern end of the Rupel Pass, through which he flew at about 1,500 feet. As he seemed unable to climb, we glided down to about 3,000 feet. As it was now getting dark, we had increasing difficulties in following either Lieut. Buchanan's or Captain Edwards's machine against the dark ground. Lieut. Buchanan was last seen by us flying low, about 3 miles west of Demirhissar station. We circled round for about 10 minutes, when we decided to return to our aerodrome. We landed at 19.30 hours.

(Signed)   A.V. Morton, Lieut. 47 Squadron.

M. MacEwan, Lieut. *do.*

The officers who were dropped had each four pigeons. One had all females and the other all males, and it was settled that if they saw they were bound to be captured, they were to let loose the pigeons at the last minute without messages. The following day two male and two female pigeons returned without messages.

Later on, when the fighting was over, the Royal Air Force officers imprisoned at Philippopolis gradually returned to the British lines. One of the first to come in was Lieutenant Buchanan, who made the following report on his adventures:—

I left Janes aerodrome at 17.00 hours on the 19th September, 1918, with a sergeant who was to be landed near Petric, and crossed the enemy lines at 18.00 hours at about 11,000 to 12,000 feet. I circled over the town of Petric several times and eventually selected a suitable spot to land about 4 miles due north of the town. I planed down and made a good landing in a field, but unfortunately a party of German troops proceeding along the Petric–Strumica road, whom I had not seen, had apparently noticed my approach and taken cover behind trees and hedges. As soon as I touched the ground, they immediately opened fire at about 600 yards to 700 yards range. My passenger at once got out of the machine and ran off towards some bushes, pursued by a party of Germans.

I then got out of the machine myself and started my engine, hich had stopped on landing; I also threw out the cage containing pigeons. I managed to take off and climbed to about 3,000 feet when my engine commenced to give trouble. I tried again and again to gain height to enable me to clear the Beles mountains, but I was obliged to descend and landed a second time, between Petric and Marinopolje. My engine then suddenly 'picked up' and I again took off but could only reach 800 feet, at which height I essayed to travel through the Rupel Pass in order to avoid the hills. I had only covered a short distance when my engine completely gave out and I was forced to glide down and crashed in the bed of the river, having had one wheel shot away and two rifle bullets through a cylinder, presumably at my first landing. Bulgarian soldiers rushed towards me shouting 'Bulgar or English?'

On telling them that I was English they fired at me at point-blank range, but the firing was very wild and the shots went in all directions, leaving me untouched. As they continued to fire I ran towards the hills, hoping to find cover, but they came after me and I was very soon overtaken as I was hampered by the extra flying clothes I was wearing. I caught hold of the nearest soldier, gripping him by the shoulders, and called upon the others to stop firing. I handed my revolver to this man, but he immediately dropped it, being afraid of it. The others then came up and went through all my pockets, but only cleared my cigarette case. They then conducted me to a Regimental H.Q. at Vetrina. Here I was examined by several Bulgar officers. Their questions were chiefly confined to the dispositions of troops, and nothing was asked regarding the R.A.F. I was particularly struck by the extraordinary efficiency of their intelligence staff work—they seemed to possess accurate information of regiments both in the front line and in reserve. The interpreter, a man who professed to be an American but spoke very bad English, several times became very annoyed at my inability to understand him. He continually accused me of telling falsehoods. On the conclusion of my interrogation, I was bound with thick rope and placed in a garry which took me to a Divisional H.Q. at Yenikoj. Here I was again examined by several Bulgar civilian judges. They questioned me as regards the Doiran battle and seemed particularly anxious to know the whereabouts of the 28th Division. They persisted in telling me that we were being beaten in what they described as 'the great Doiran battle.' They asked me whether I knew if the French were going to attack on the Struma front. No questions were asked about the R.A.F. When asked if I knew what would happen to me, and on my replying in the negative, I was informed that in all probability I should be shot as a spy. I told them that as I was wearing my King's uniform, they could not do this according to international law, but they replied it was not a Bulgarian law.

I was then placed in a dug-out guarded by three sentries; where I spent the night. The following morning, 20th instant, I left in a motorcar for Army Headquarters at Sveti Vrac. On arrival there I was immediately taken before a German staff officer, who asked every kind of question possible, as to the dispositions of troops, organisation of R.A.F., and also the exact position of British G.H.Q. and the name of the 'General in Chief.'

As an example of their up-to-date information regarding R.A.F., when I was questioned about Marian Aerodrome, and

OBLIQUE PHOTOGRAPH OF THE RUPEL PASS

gave evasive answers, I was told it was useless to lie, as they had already full information, and produced photographs of this aerodrome, showing 5 machines on the ground, and of Amberkoj and of Salonika, taken only a very few days previously. Every attempt was made to catch me out, and on one occasion he was successful. I was asked if I had been out on this front any length of time, and I told him I had only just arrived. Later he asked me if I knew Lieut. Gaynor, and on my replying that we were in the same squadron he said, 'Well, that officer has been out here 9 months, so I suppose you have too.'

The following day, 21st, I was taken before a Bulgar major who asked me very nearly the same questions as I had been asked on the previous day. He asked me about G.H.Q. again and what type of man General Milne was, as they wanted to go down at once and see him! He informed me that I had been playing a dangerous game and must know what to expect. The interpreter on this occasion was a doctor who spoke very good English.

Several days later I was taken before a court consisting of 4 Bulgar civilian judges, about 20 other officers being present. Exactly the same questions were asked as on the two previous occasions.

Whilst at Sveti Vrac I was kept in a cell about 6 feet square and guarded by 4 sentries. I was very badly fed, being given only one loaf (black bread) and some water in 6 days. On one occasion two Bulgar aviators came from Sveti Vrac aerodrome to see me and permission was given for them to take me to their aerodrome. Here I was treated quite well, being given a good meal and plenty to drink, but I strongly suspected that this was in expectation of getting more out of me. I remained at the acrodrome until the evening, during which time I was shown round their sheds, workshops, and machines. They continually asked me questions as regards number and type of British machines, quality of pilots, and ground organisation; number of lorries, cars, etc., in units and details of photographic work, e.g. in what particular light, if any, did we develop plates? They also questioned me about the Greek squadron, about which I professed to, and, as a matter of fact, did know little.

At the end of 12 days I was taken on a bullock wagon to Porna and thence by train to Drama, Zanthi, Dedeagatch, Adrianople, and Philippopolis. On arrival at Philippopolis I was placed in the Prisoners-of-War Camp, where I met a number of other British officers. The camp was enclosed in barbed wire in close strands, which was removed when they heard of the possible arrival of British troops.

Just before I left Sveti Vrac, I was informed that I need not worry, as it had been decided that I would not be shot. This was, as far as I could ascertain, owing to the intervention of the American representative at Sofia, and to the refusal of certain high Bulgar officials to consent to such a decision.

The arrival of the American representative at Sveti Vrac caused much excitement among the Bulgars, and when I saw him, he told me that peace or an armistice would shortly be declared.

About the same time, I noticed from my cell that a quantity of the civil population were streaming northwards, apparently taking all their household goods with them. On one occasion I saw what appeared to be British troops marching N. in column of route, and I shouted to them, but they took no notice and I afterwards learnt that they were Russian soldiers (presumably prisoners) wearing uniform and sun helmets of English pattern, probably originally supplied by us.

Everywhere the Bulgars seemed in great fear of our machines, and on one occasion of a bombing raid on Livunovo while I was at Sveti Vrac, everybody disappeared into dug-outs, taking me with them. About the 13th of October the American representative informed us at Philippopolis that we were to leave for Salonika in parties, and I eventually reported to 16th Wing on the 15th of October.

The Franco-Serbian forces, we have seen, got through to the Vardar line of communications by September the 21st, thus turning the whole of the Doiran front. This success, be it repeated, was greatly helped because the British, by their feint attacks of September the 1st and their main attacks of September the 18th and 19th, had pinned the chief enemy reserves to the Doiran front.

An army reconnaissance by 47 on the morning of the 21st established without any doubt the fact of the enemy's retreat. The report of this reconnaissance which is given below showed that some 500 lorries were moving through the defile west of Rabrovo; that all the hangars had been removed from Hudova which for two years had been the centre of most of the aerial activity by the Germans on the

Doiran front; that the Demirkapu Dump had been abandoned; and that various dumps were already on fire.

The report reads:—

Copy Extract from War Diary of 16th Wing R.A.F.

No. of Recc.	Date	Aeroplane Type	Aeroplane No.	Squadron	Pilot	Observer	Reference Maps	Hour commenced	Hour concluded
J.784	21.9.18	D.H.9 D.H.9	6236 6217	47	Capt. J. R. Milne Lieut. A. V. Morton	Lieut. J. C. F. Holland Lieut. M. MacEwan	1,200,000 Vodesa	08.30	12.00

Time.	Places.	Observation.
		Page No.

ARMY RECONNAISSANCE.

Left to reconnoitre STRUMICA Valley—NEGOTIN—HUDOVA.

Time.	Places.	Observation.
08.30	HAJDARLI	Camps same as reported on 20.9.18.
10.00	STRUMICA Valley	Sheds and stacks in dump are burning. No trains observed.
10.35	CASTROVO	
10.40	RABROVO	The defile W. of RABROVO on the STRUMICA-RABROVO road was packed with transport, and round RABROVO were anything up to 500 lorries and H.T. wagons waiting to go up the road.
10.45	HUDOVA	All hangars have been removed from the Aerodrome, only hessoneaux and sheds remaining. Sheds and stacks in station are burning. Large numbers of transport on road between here and CASTROVO proceeding E. 1 train coming S. from DEMIR KAPU proceeding E. About 5 trains in the Station. Some H.T. coming S. to the station.
10.50	DEMIR KAPU	Road down gorge had large numbers of wagons going S. The dump is abandoned. Hospital marquees have been removed. Stacks have been removed, leaving bare patches. No trains in station. Sheds only standing. No fires.
11.00	DEMIR KAPU—NEGOTIN	
11.15	KAIVOLAK	No move of any kind. Small trenches can be seen in this area. No shelling. 4 trains, 2 very long, one off rails, and the other burning. Station burning. Several H.T. and horsemen and 6 lorries between here and NEGOTIN appeared to be halted.
11.30	HUDOVA	An enormous fire could be seen from here, presumably at GRADSKO.
11.45	HUDOVA—MIROVCE	The road N.E. from HUDOVA station to KOSTURINO is not much used, only 15 H.T. being observed going N.E. About 50 H.T. halted in Dero N. of the station. 2 very long trains no engines. About 100 lorries passing towards HUDOVA station and crossing HUDOVA bridge.
11.47	MIRAVINCA	
11.50	VARDARIORE—PARDQVICA	Slight transport E. to CASTROVO. Hospital still standing.
12.00	HAJDARLI	No trains, dump appears deserted, stacks removed. Hospital removed. Returned.

(Sgd.) J. C. F. HOLLAND, Lieut.
(Sgd.) MacEwan, Lieut. M.

THE KOSTURINO PASS SHOWING RETREATING BULGARS WHO WERE AFTERWARDS BOMBED.

The information contained in this report was supplemented and confirmed by other observers and, as an immediate result, the XII Corps H.Q. ordered all work on defensive lines to be stopped and all troops to be given a short rest preparatory to a rapid advance.

Meantime there was no rest for the Royal Air Force or for the Bulgar. As one pilot put it, the officers of 47 "had the time of their lives." The enemy retreating along the Vardar Valley-Cestovo-Kosturino roads offered an excellent target. The Bulgar Army was so thoroughly demoralised as to offer little or no fire to our machines, and the German air force had disappeared from the front. Our machines flew over in relays, and from low heights exhausted the ammunition from their machine-guns against the unhappy Bulgar and bombed the columns of his transport, causing endless confusion. In many places the roads run alongside ravines and whole masses of transport were blown down these ravines, to crash in the gully below.

At other points the roads cut through the mountain-side, and bombs dropped here piled twisted lorries and dead animals and men high on one another, blocking the way to the oncoming columns, which, ever pressing on from the rear, blocked the line backwards. These congested, panic-stricken masses offered still better targets to our machines, of which every advantage was taken. Throughout the next few days, the enemy fled over the mountain-paths, leaving a trail of abandoned stores and guns, burning dumps and tumbled transport and dead behind him. He was closely pursued by the British infantry and forestalled by the Royal Air Force. Possibly the worst execution of all was done in the Kosturino Pass, which was the only line of retreat open to the enemy after the fall of the Vardar line.

This narrow defile very quickly became choked with troops. Photographs taken from the air show the road to be a continuous line of dots which look for all the world like an enormous trek of ants. The first raid on these columns took place on the morning of the 21st, when twenty-five machines dropped 5,096 lb. of high explosive and fired some twelve thousand rounds of ammunition. Thence the machines returned and filled up again and continued the destruction.

On the 26th of September officers from 47 Squadron were sent by car to report on the condition of the road to Kosturino which had been captured the day before. Their description of the destruction to Bulgar transport and personnel caused by the bomb-raids on the 21st and 22nd was remarkable, and the following telegram, forwarded on the 26th of September by advanced XVI Corps to advanced G.H.Q., testifies to the enormous damage, both actual and moral, done to the retreating columns.

> The routes from Cestovo Valley to Kosturino show signs of indescribable confusion that must have existed in the retreat of Bulgar Army AAA Guns of all kinds, motorcars, machine-guns, rifles, and every kind of war material abandoned AAA Dead animals are strewn everywhere AAA Indicating that our R.A.F. must have contributed largely to bring about this state of things.

Similar havoc was caused in the Kresna pass, a deep, narrow gorge on the Struma River, the only line of retreat open to the enemy. Here, on the 27th, 28th, and 29th of September, massed columns of all arms, which in the narrow defile were unable to escape off the road, presented wonderful targets to flights of bombing machines sent over in relays, The day of greatest destruction was the 28th of September, when 47 Squadron registered fifty-seven hours flying time in bomb and machine-gun attacks on the Kresna pass and Gjujsevo.

This brilliant and rapid advance of the Allies finished the Bulgarian army, which pleaded for peace.

On the 26th of September a Bulgarian major, carrying despatches, motored under a white flag to the British lines on the Strumica road and, after being brought to advanced British G.H.Q. at Janes, was taken on to Salonika.

On the 28th of September two motorcars containing Bulgarian envoys under large white flags passed through the British lines and were watched with interest by Major Bates and other 47 Squadron officers who were looking for advanced landing-grounds in the Strumica and Bosiljevo district. These envoys were taken to Salonika, and finally, in the early hours of the 30th of September, the news of the armistice reached the squadron in the form of the following telegram, to receive which the squadron commander was awakened without ceremony from his sleep:—

> By reason of the Convention which has just been signed hostilities with the Bulgarian Army will cease at midday on Monday, 30th Sept. AAA All troops on both sides will remain where they are AAA No further attack will be initiated by us after the receipt of this message AAA Bulgarian troops will be warned by parliamentaires from our troops in the line. 12th Corps 02.15.

Thus was the Bulgarian Army saved from a military disaster on

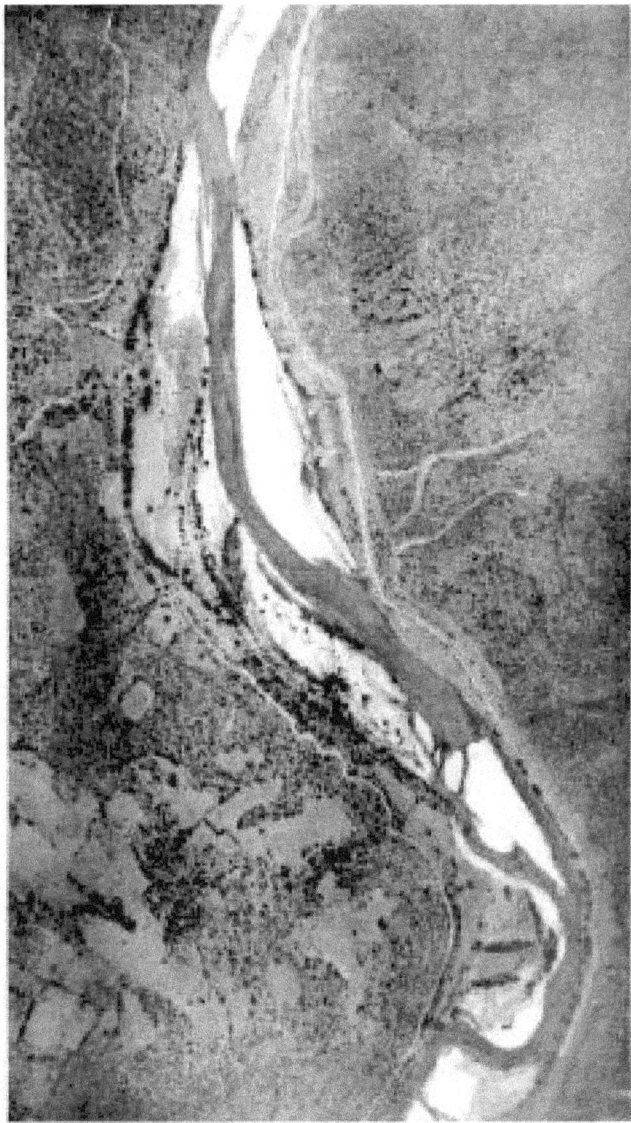

A PORTION OF THE KRESNA SHOWING A CONTINUOUS STREAM OF TRANSPORT.
One of a sequence of 25 taken at 9 a.m. on September 29th; each portion of the road tells the same story.
The retreating enemy were heavily bombed and indescribable havoc caused.

a vast scale. Following the Bulgarian armistice, quick communication with Sofia presented great difficulty. This was solved by a daily service of D.H.9.'s run by "A" Flight 47 Squadron, which continued working to and from Sofia most successfully for several weeks, carrying despatches and staff officers until reconstruction of road and rail made this unnecessary. Besides the Sofia detachment, 47 Squadron maintained during October a detachment at Drama as an advanced landing-ground *en route* for Dedeagatch. From Drama a 47 reconnaissance party pushed on to Gumuldzina, being received there by the Bulgar general as the first British troops to arrive. A landing-ground was found at Gumuldzina, and two A.W. machines from "B" Flight 47 Squadron landed there on the 25th of October, being followed by two scout machines from 150 Squadron to make up a mixed detachment for operations in Turkey.

From Gumuldzina aerial reconnaissance was extended to Adrianople and eastwards over Turkey, and on the 28th of October the detachment moved on to Dedeagatch. Operations ended with the news of Turkey's surrender on the 30th of October, and the Dedeagatch R.A.F. detachment was recalled to Salonika on the 10th of November.

During December two D.H.9 machines from "A" Flight 47 carried despatches from Salonika to Bucharest, the capital of Roumania, thus making the fifth great Balkan state visited by 47 Squadron machines during the last months of the war and the armistice period.

After years of waiting, of fighting, and living under difficult conditions, and without that sympathy from the people at home which compensates a soldier for many hardships, the Salonika army had the satisfaction of knowing that its blow at the Bulgarian Army had dislodged the keystone of the German structure, which was soon itself to come tumbling down. The officers of the Royal Air Force were able to land at Hudova and inspect some of the country which, although it was known so well, had been forbidden land for so long. A feature of the final operations was the devotion to duty of the N.C.O.'s and men of the squadron. They worked continuously night and day on their machines. They seemed not to want any rest. The weather was exceptionally hot, and there were many instances of men, suffering from severe attacks of malaria, who refused to report sick, so that whilst they could still get about, they might keep their engines and machines serviceable.

The history of the squadron on the Macedonian front has no very fantastic pages. It is mostly a story of good comradeship. The spirit of the squadron never burned more brightly than in the days that marked the close of a tedious campaign. 47 was a happy brotherhood, instinct with high ideals, and living in the peaceful atmosphere of work well done. Its members received a great trust—to forge a link in the tradition of a new service. They did their duty, and for those who fell the monument which will endure is not above their graves, but in the memory of those who have the future of the squadron in their keeping.

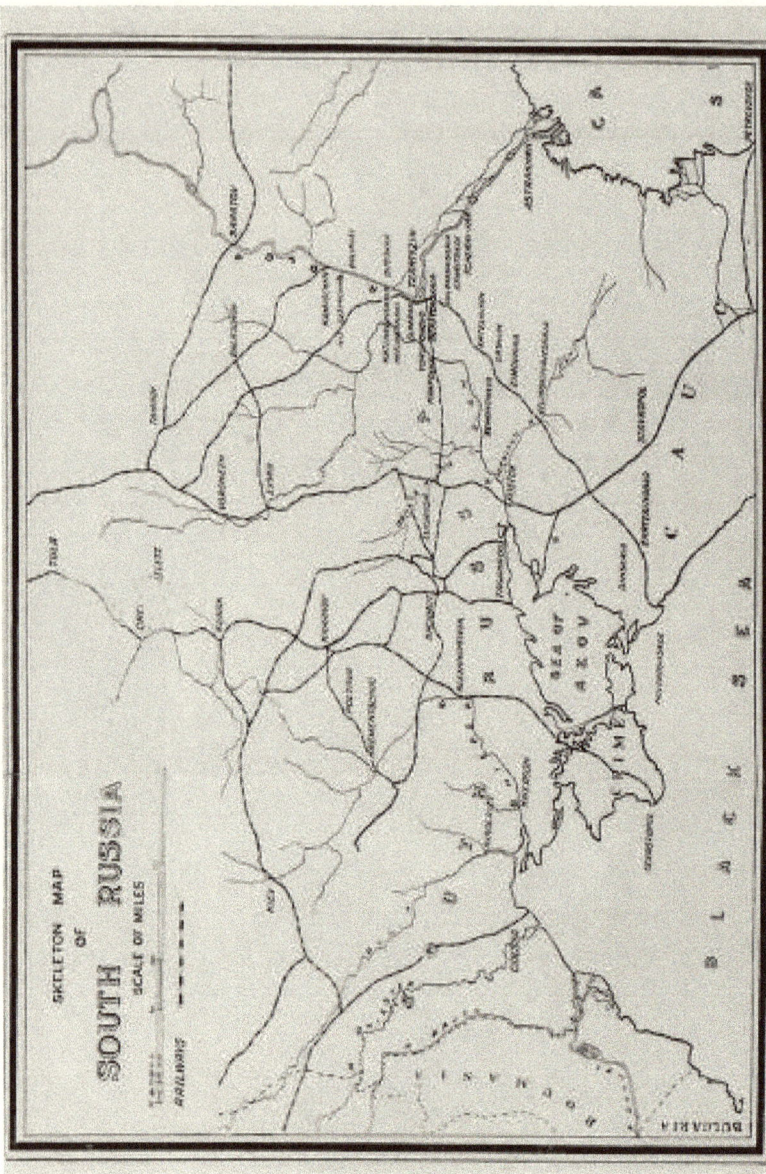

SKELETON MAP
OF
SOUTH RUSSIA

SCALE OF MILES

RAILWAYS

BLACK SEA

SEA OF AZOV

CAUCASUS

ROUMANIA

BULGARIA

Part 2: South Russia

CHAPTER 10

Denikin's Campaign

The early exploits of the Russian Volunteer Army are full of wonder. The story of Denikin is an epic story. In his offensive, lasting some five months between April and October 1919, Denikin took a quarter of a million of prisoners, 700 guns—1,700 machine guns, 35 armoured trains, and long lists of rolling-stock. His "push" took him as far as Orel, which is only some 200 miles from Moscow. In those few months his armies swept over an area 850 miles one way and 250 the other: his "front" had extended from one of 600 miles to one over double the length. His very success had in it the germs of his downfall. The peasants in the emancipated towns knew all the horrors of the Bolshevik regime. The volunteer army was welcomed, and the peasants expected that those necessaries of life which had now become to them something more than luxuries would once again become available. Instead, they found new land laws coming into force which compelled them to give up a portion of their sunflower seeds, etc., to the legal holder of the land which they had seized.

There were heavy requisitions on the part of the Volunteer Army. There was looting by the Cossacks—and there were excesses by both the Cossacks and volunteers. There were intrigues and political jealousies and administrative incapacity. Indeed, the liberated peasants found themselves bitterly disillusioned. Thus, the ground was ripe for propaganda. This propaganda was most ably conducted by the Soviet Government. It was systematic and widespread and inordinately clever. It was lavish in promises which were of as little value as the rouble notes which paid for the spreading of them. Then there were typhus and other epidemics. Denikin had not the wherewithal to keep his army clean, and fever cut lanes of desolation across his ranks.

The story of his force is a story of great heroism side by side with extreme squalor, of almost superhuman powers of endurance often ending in unnameable privations and cruelty. It is not easy to summarise the complicated South Russian campaign in a few sentences, yet some sort of summary must be attempted if the work of 47 Squadron in that theatre is to be understood. The Russian revolution of March, 1917, seriously weakened the Russian Army. The Bolshevik *coup d'état* finished it. This was in November of the same year. From the ashes of the old army there arose a volunteer force on the shore of the Black Sea. This force, under the command of General Alexieff, was mostly recruited from officers of the now dead Imperial army. Mobilising against it were the soldiers of the Soviet Government— the Red Army.

Alexieff organised his destitute rabble into a disciplined force, but before they were seriously tested death took him from his command and General A. I. Denikin succeeded him. And so, we come to the end of the year 1918, when peace was already settling down on Western Europe. The Soviet Government wanted the Ukraine—the granary of Europe; they wanted also the rich Donetz basin. Accordingly, they marshalled their strong and well-equipped forces, and by the end of the year were facing the armies of the Ukraine from Kiev to Kharkov: the Cossacks of the Don, led by Krasnoff, leading away from the Ukrainians right to the Volga at Tsaritsin, and covering the Donetz area; and from there south to the Caucasus the volunteers under Wrangel. The attack was launched. The Ukrainians gave way rapidly. The Cossacks, victims of a subtle propaganda, were broken.

The volunteers fought to better purpose. By February, 1919, this army had effected an immense left wheel and had brought its right flank on to the Caspian coast and its front on to the Manich river, facing north-east. For some months the activity centred around the Donetz basin. In the meantime, preparations, both by the Bolsheviks and by the volunteer commanders, were being made for a decisive struggle in the spring. In the desultory fighting which went on during the early months of 1919, the Bolsheviks had the advantage. They had advanced down the Volga to a point 60 miles south of Tsaritsin and had opened that river for the passage of their destroyers to Astrakhan. Denikin decided to attack Tsaritsin, not only because of its value as a key to the Volga, but also because he hoped to join up with Kolchak *via* Tsaritsin and Saratov.

The advance met with success, and although there were disquieting features, such as the evacuation of Odessa in April, the risings of the Chechen tribesmen, which threatened his right flank, and the unrest in Georgia. Denikin had every reason to be satisfied when in

June Kharkov and Tsaritsin were taken. The advance was to continue. Wrangel was ordered to advance his line to Saratov-Balashov by the 24th of July. Prudence might have dictated consolidation rather than further commitments. But Denikin had little choice. It was a case for a rapid and decisive advance or failure. He had no sure economic basis on which to build his strategic plans. He made no attempt to hold a continuous line, but operated with mobile columns. He was well supplied with rifles and ammunition, but could not use many men from the liberated areas owing to his lack of clothing and boots.

Towards the end of July, the threat to Denikin's right flank had developed. He had lost a naval engagement on the Caspian, and the whole situation on the Astrakhan front was disquieting. However, by the end of July, Kamishin and Poltava had been taken. But the men were now fighting in rags and bare feet. Medical comforts were missing, and it was obvious that although the spirit of the men remained remarkably good, they could not go on indefinitely under these conditions.

Nor was the Soviet Government inactive. Alarmed by the advance, they were massing further troops from the Siberian front. Still Denikin went on, and by September the 6th had captured Kiev, the capital of the Ukraine.

But General Denikin was uneasy. The acclamations of the population of Kiev did not blind him to the precariousness of his position. He had only two weak corps to hold the country up to Kiev and only one mixed corps to continue the offensive on that front. Along his lines of communication there were roving armed bands looting and destroying. Orel, the northernmost town to be captured by the volunteer army, fell on October the 13th, and Denikin's bolt was shot. By the end of October, he had evacuated Orel, Voronejh, and Liski. On the Volga front the moral of Wrangel's troops was good and the work of British airmen had created a fine feeling of comradeship.

Wrangel freely attributed a great share in the defence of Tsaritsin and the subsequent successful operations to daring and skilful low flying against enemy troops, especially cavalry, who were repeatedly dispersed with loss. The Bolshevik Volga flotilla of forty-two craft, a serious menace, was also repeatedly attacked by bombing machines and suffered great losses. The Bolshevik advance became increasingly serious. Denikin's armies fought well, but were remorselessly pushed back, and, with the fall of Kiev before Christmas, his failing fortunes became apparent to the world. As his centre was pushed back, so Denikin had to withdraw his wings. So, it was Wrangel had to evacuate Tsaritsin, the scene of great heroism and greater sacrifice.

By the end of March all was over. After a gallant stand, and harried by all sorts of local levies, Denikin had managed to evacuate refugees and the remnants of his army *via* Novorossisk, which the Bolsheviks entered on March the 27th, 1920. Denikin himself went to Constantinople and thence to England.

CHAPTER 11

47 In South Russia

The history of 47 Squadron in South Russia does not cover the whole period of Denikin's campaign. The squadron, as shall be told hereafter, was bombing the Bolshevik Armies in June and continued to do good work until October, when officially No. 47 Squadron ceased to exist in South Russia. Many members of the squadron however, remained as volunteers under Denikin and did invaluable work until the evacuation.

We must go back to the days following the Bulgarian collapse, so as to follow the fortunes of the squadron in their due order. When the war with Bulgaria was concluded, the machines of 47 were thoroughly overhauled, and the squadron held itself in readiness for any emergency. Orders were at first received to prepare for a move northwards to the Danube, but these were cancelled and further instructions issued for a move eastwards to the Turkish frontier. All Bulgarian aerodromes were placed at the disposal of Allied aviators, and some of them were used, from which reconnaissances of the Turkish area were made.

A composite flight of two A.W.'s from 47, and four Sopwith Camels from 150 Squadron, left Salonika on October the 25th, 1918, for an aerodrome previously selected by Captain J. R. Milne, southeast of Gumuldzina. This aerodrome, called Demirbilji, was some 20 miles from Dedeagatch, on the railway line to Constantinople. On October the 29th this composite flight moved to an aerodrome east of Dedeagatch, but two days later hostilities with Turkey ceased at midday. However, this flight remained near Dedeagatch until November the 23rd, doing occasional reconnaissances.

It then moved to Salonika. Meantime the remainder of 47 Squadron moved as follows:—"A" Flight from Hajdarli to Salonika on October the 20th, 1918, and "B" Flight on November the 3rd. "C" Flight remained at Janes until February 16th, 1919, when they moved with headquarters to Amberkoi. The two flights from Salonika had moved up to this aerodrome earlier in the month, and so, by the end of February, the whole squadron was concentrated there. The work of the squadron after the signing of the armistice with Bulgaria had mostly been the conveying of staff and intelligence officers to such places as Sofia, so that the business of consolidating the peace could proceed with the least avoidable loss of time. It should be remembered that there were no railways, and that in many cases bridges had been destroyed. The journey to Sofia over the bad Bulgarian roads, even under normal conditions, would have taken considerable time and patience.

At the end of February, then, No. 47 were at Amberkoi, sitting, Micawber-like, waiting for something to turn up.

Meantime the British Government had decided to give support to General Denikin in his fight against the Soviet Government in South Russia, and No. 47 Squadron were chosen as part of the Royal Air Force contribution to that campaign. On April the 16th the personnel of one flight of 47 left Salonika for Novorossisk, South Russia. The following officers went:—

Captain H. G. Davis.
Lieutenant C. H. Jones.
Lieutenant E. C. White.
2nd Lieutenant A. M. Verity.
2nd Lieutenant C. C. Reynolds.
Lieutenant D. B. Thomson.
Lieutenant R. Addison.
Lieutenant M. MacEwan.
2nd Lieutenant C. P. Primrose.
Lieutenant L. Watman technical officer
2nd Lieutenant A. Gold *ditto*

On April the 20th the following officers were transferred from No. 17 Squadron to 47 and left for Novorossisk:—

2nd Lieutenant R. Walker.
2nd Lieutenant H. S. Laidlaw.
2nd Lieutenant G. B. Hopwood.
Captain N. Greenslade.
2nd Lieutenant H. Mercer.

On April the 29th these officers followed:—

Captain F. W. Hudson.

Captain S. G. Frogley.

2nd Lieutenant B. Dumas.

2nd Lieutenant E. A. Burridge.

2nd Lieutenant W. Mann.

Meantime the first shipment of machines, stores, and transport for 47 was sent by the S.S. *Warpointer* to Novorossisk on April the 24th. Novorossisk is a well-equipped port on the Black Sea. It was a great grain and cement shipping centre. From it railways run *via* Ekaterinodar, north round the Sea of Azov to the Great Don port of Rostov; northeast to Tsaritsin on the Volga; and east following the feet of the Caucasian mountains to Petrovsk on the Caspian. Meantime such of the remainder of No. 47 as were not demobilised or posted elsewhere gradually got through to South Russia, and on May the 28th, 1919, the squadron was struck off the strength of 16th Wing.

During the time that it was in South Russia, No. 47 Squadron was under Major R. Collishaw, who took command of it on the 13th of June, 1919, and remained with it until the 31st of March, 1920. For part of the time covered by his command, the unit was not known as 47 Squadron, but had another title. Major Collishaw had already had a great career with the R.N.A.S. and R.A.F. in France, and consequently brought all the strength of his personality to the squadron. He had collected a party of officers and men in England and took them out to South Russia *via* Constantinople.

His party included many famous pilots and mechanics who were keen for hard work and adventure. They were, before the campaign ended, to need all their skill and faith and courage. With 7 officers and 179 other ranks of his party, Major Collishaw arrived at Ekaterinodar on July the 11th. The aerodrome at Ekaterinodar was a large, flat, muddy surface near the racecourse. It was shared with Russian aviators until October, when the British finally moved up to Beketovka.

Headquarters of the squadron remained at Ekaterinodar, and from here in June "C" Flight was equipped and sent up to the Volga front to operate against Tsaritsin.

In the early part of the month the *War Foam* and *War Celt* arrived at Novorossisk with stores, personnel, and aeroplanes, and these were disembarked and hangars were erected at Ekaterinodar to receive them. All this work was done on rations that were not exactly good, and there is an illuminative note in the *War Diary* to the effect that "a strong complaint was made to Headquarters *re* rations."

"C" Flight moved towards the Volga front on June the 10th. Five machines left at a quarter to eight in the morning for Velikoknyajeskaya, which is situated some 180 miles from Ekaterinodar on the railway to Tsaritsin, and on a tributary of the marshy Manich. Four of these machines arrived safely at their destination, but one fell by the wayside. This one came down at Dinskaya owing to engine trouble, and crashed in a cornfield. The occupants, Lieutenants E. C. White and J. N. Webb, were unhurt, but owing to the disturbed state of the country, and their ignorance of Russian, their prospect of salving the machine and feeding themselves was not too bright.

However, Lieutenant Dumas, the equipment officer, left Ekaterinodar with a small party to salve the machine. They spent the night at Dinskaya, some 20 miles from headquarters, and after adventures with the municipal transport of the local village they managed to get the machine to the railway line. They then commandeered the next express down to the base and held up the whole of the train service of South Russia for some hours whilst they loaded up the machine.

Lieutenant Dumas in a letter home tells the story of this episode:—

I had a little change the other day. One of our machines left here to go off up the line, but had to come down owing to engine trouble. The pilot very sensibly landed just along the railway line. He managed (somehow), not knowing any Russian, to get a message to us telling us where he was. It was only about fifteen miles away, so I had a shot to get there by road— but we only got about three miles before the road completely ceased. We had to turn back, go to the railway station and get a closed truck and a flat put on the next train. We eventually arrived about half-past five, got our truck, etc., put in a siding at the nearest station, went down to the machine on a railwayman's trolley.

We worked all that evening while the pilot, White, went down to the village to get some accommodation for us. He eventually, with the help of a lady who spoke French, found a lodging; as far as I could understand, a house kept for the purpose and paid for by the government. When we had finished, owing to it growing dark, we went off to the place while the men went to a farmhouse near. They gave us an excellent meal, heaps of eggs, butter, and milk, but no tea or sugar. According to what I can hear, it is the same all over the country, masses to eat in the country places, but they refuse to sell it in the towns because they do not trust the paper money used everywhere. We had to sleep on the floor, but I was so tired I did not mind.

Next morning for breakfast again an enormous dish of fried eggs—about eighteen for three of us, beautiful white bread and butter, and fresh milk. Then began the struggle. What I had to do was to get an engine from the railway people, run the flat down the line and get enough men to hoist the machine on to it. After an hour's fierce argument—I had an interpreter with me—we managed to stop the next train going through and commandeer the engine. So far so good, though what the passengers on the train thought I don't know. However, we only had the engine for three hours. I got the labour off the Ataman of the village, twenty stout Cossacks, and started off down the line. When we got to the place, the men (our own men) were all ready for us. Then came the crux. The flat was quite four feet high and the aeroplane weighed about a ton.

It was a desperate struggle, only solved by using the door of the closed truck as an approach. It took us a good half-hour by sheer pushing. Just as we were really getting near the top, the end of the platform which dropped down broke and got jammed—one wheel of the machine on it and the other wheel pushing against the under-side. At this moment the Russians said we must move. It was only a single line, and a train was coming. I said the train must wait, and we all heaved. After about ten minutes really pushing our souls out, she went over and sat all right. In ten minutes more her planes, etc., were packed alongside and we started off back to the station. I gave the Russians back their engine, and the train we had kept standing engineless was able to proceed.

It was now about half-past one. Some went off back for lunch. . . . We had a very good meal indeed—a broth of sorts, then meat and strawberries and cream. . . . We collected our kit and wanted to pay, but they refused to take any money, saying that we had come to Russia to help them and they were honoured to be able to do anything for us. We tried hard to make them take some money, but they absolutely refused. ... In the towns nobody likes us, nor is willing to do very much for us. In the country, apparently, things are very different. Our own men had also been looked after exceedingly well. . . ."

The four machines of "C" Flight which had landed at Velikokn-yajeskaya were, according to original instructions, to proceed to Ra-montnaya, a further 140 miles on their journey, but it was discovered that the railway bridges *en route* were broken. The first broken bridge was east of Gashun, over the river which takes its name from that town. Accordingly, a reconnaissance was made and a site chosen at Zimovnika near Gashun. The difficulty now was to arrange with the Russian railway authorities to get the train of "C" Flight through to this place, some 55 miles away. In the result the train left at 5 o'clock in the morning of the 12th, and the 55 miles had been completed by 6 p.m. the same evening, which cannot be called an express service. When the flight arrived, communication was at once established with the headquarters of the Caucasian Army at Katelnikov, some distance up the line, and a promise received that the train would be one of the first to go through after the bridge had been repaired. No information could be obtained by the flight as to the position at the front. No one knew whether Tsaritsin had been taken or not.

The flight remained at Zimovnika until the 15th. In the afternoon of this day the bridge was opened and the R.A.F. train put sixth on the list, passing forward at midnight. The machines left on the fol-lowing morning. During the few days at Zimovnika the weather was execrable. It rained constantly and the resultant conditions were most uncomfortable.

On the 16th the train of "C" Flight arrived at Katelnikov at three in the afternoon. There was no aerodrome at this station, and although the ground was flat there were earth-bumps about 18 inches high dotted at intervals of a few yards. Consequently, one machine crashed on landing, breaking the under-carriage, the port aileron and the tail-skid. During the afternoon there was torrential rain, which continued all night, and on the following morning the aerodrome was water-logged. Although it was impossible to get a D.H.9 off the ground, three were loaded with bombs in readiness for when things cleared up. The time was spent in erecting tents.

On the 19th Lieutenant E. C. White and Lieutenant Webb arrived at Katelnikov from Ekaterinodar. On June the 20th, the second dam-aged bridge was completed and the flight left for Gniloaksaiskaya. This village is some 60 miles from Tsaritsin, and it was from here that "C" Flight did its work against the Volga front. Lieutenant Clavey crashed at the aerodrome on landing. Continuous rain fell throughout these days, but on the 22nd a raid with four machines was attempted in the afternoon against Tsaritsin. After 25 miles had been flown, the weather got so bad that it was impossible to see anything, a blanket of thick clouds closing round from the ground and extending up to 10,000 feet. The machines therefore turned back. Lieutenant Reynolds crashed on landing, owing to the very gusty wind that was blowing.

On the 23rd, however, the first raid was carried out. Three machines left at 10.30 a.m. with sixteen 20-lb. and two 112-lb. bombs. The objective was the South-Eastern railway station at Tsaritsin. The machines arrived safely and bombs were dropped from a height of 5,000 feet, doing damage to the station buildings, rolling-stock, and neighbouring houses. In addition, about a 1,000 rounds were fired into barges on the Volga, the station, on streets, and on some cavalry near Elshanka. The raid was led by Captain Davis, who was in command of "C" Flight. The other two pilots were Lieutenants White and Verity and the observers Lieutenants Thompson, MacEwan, and 2nd Lieutenant Mann.

A word is due here on Captain Davis. He was one of the original observers of No. 47 Squadron, joining the squadron in its early days in Salonika. He did excellent work over the Vardar front and was often chosen for the most difficult jobs. After a spell on that front, he went to Egypt and qualified as a pilot. He returned to the squadron in 1918. He was a quiet, intense, stout-hearted officer. He was sound rather than brilliant, and much of the fine work done by "C" Flight in South Russia can be traced back to his example. After he left the Royal Air Force, when fighting had ceased, he went to Africa and (I am informed) died there, soon after his arrival, of blackwater fever.

On June the 24th Captain Davis led another raid on Tsaritsin with good results.

I cannot do better than give the extracts from the squadron war diary for this time. This will show in brief form what "C" Flight did towards the capture of Tsaritsin.

24th June, 1919. Low clouds in morning. Clear in afternoon. Three machines left for Tsaritsin and bombed barges alongside wharf, neighbouring houses, and houses in vicinity of S.E. station. 450 rds. S.A.A. fired into barges, wharves, and streets. Machines returned 18.10 hrs. Pilots, Capt. Davis, Lt. White, and Lt. Clavey. Observers, 2/Lt. Primrose, Lt. Webb, Lt. Hopwood.

25th June, 1919. Morning very cloudy. Afternoon fairly clear. Two machines left at 15.10 hrs. for bomb-raid on Tsaritsin-Dubovka-Kachalinskaya-Tsaritsin. Two 112-lb. bombs in main street, 8 20-lb. bombs in various parts of town and station. Roads to Dubovka found clear. Isolated groups of horses between Dubovka and Kachalinskaya. Considerable concentration of troops, and movement of convoys along road and railway line between Kachalinskaya and Tsaritsin. Machines returned 17.45. 300 rds. S.A.A. fired into cavalry and convoys. Pilots, Lt. Verity and Lt. Reynolds. Observers, Lt. Thompson and Lt. Primrose.

26th June, 1919. Fine weather. Two machines—with Capt. Davis and Lt. Clavey, and Lt. Mann and Lt. Hopwood—bombed Tsaritsin at 09.00 hrs. this morning. Direct hits were obtained on the docks and one barge. Also bombs on station. Observation of exact result was difficult owing to clouds. 800 rds. S.A.A. fired by observers. 8 20-lb. and 2 112-lb. bombs dropped. At 16.10 hrs. three machines, with pilots Lt. White, Lt. Verity, and Lt. Reynolds, and observers Lt. Thompson, Lt. MacEwan, and Lt. Phillip, left aerodrome to bomb Gumrak and Kotlobanski stations. 16 20-lb. and 2 112-lb. bombs dropped. Direct hits on stations, rolling-stock, and track were obtained, also on groups of cavalry and transport. One 20-lb. bomb fell in centre of group of 200 cavalry with good effect. 1,500 rds. S.A.A. fired into groups of cavalry and transport. A large concentration of enemy camps, transport, and cavalry was observed in the area Kotlobanski-Gumrak, but very little movement along roads. On returning, one blade of propeller on Lt. White's machine was found to be split from tip to boss.

27th June, 1919. Lt. Verity and Lt. Thompson flew to Ekaterinodar, journey of 340 miles, taking 3 hrs. 20 mins. At 08.25 hrs. Lt. White flew to Tcherveenaya, landed there, and took up Major Bruce of Tank Corps for reconnaissance of lines. Returned to aerodrome 12.00 hrs. At 14.00 hrs. Lt. Clavey and Lt. Hopwood left aerodrome and bombed Gumrak station and Voroponova village, which contained troops. Casualties to troops and transport were caused. Transport was parked, so effect was probably severe. Returned 16.15 hrs. 8 20-lb. bombs dropped and 500 rds. S.A.A. fired.

28th June, 1919. 2/Lt. Verity and Lt. Thompson returned from Ekaterinodar at 08.50. Time of journey 3 hrs. 40 mins. Lt. White and Lt. MacEwan left to bomb Tsaritsin at 04.30. Good effects were obtained on railway junction S. of Tsaritsin, one large shed being hit, also hits on wharf buildings and shipping on Volga. One 20-lb. bomb hit one of the tug-boats towing enemy H.Q. ship. The balloon and parent ship were also attacked. No apparent damage observed. 8 20-lb. bombs dropped and 500 rds. S.A.A. fired. Lt. White and Lt. Primrose bombed troops and transport near railway junction S. of Tsaritsin at 16.35. Damage to rolling-stock and casualties to transport caused. This evening two trucks, with pilots, observers, mechanics, bombs, and petrol, left for Tcherveenaya.

29th June, 1919. Three machines, pilots Capt. Davis, Lt. White, and 2/Lt. Verity, and observers Lt. Thompson, 2/Lt. Primrose, and 2/Lt. Mann, left to bomb Tsaritsin area at 03.20. Various direct hits and good results were obtained on troops and transport in area Tsaritsin-Grutenkaya-Gumrak. 3 112-lb. bombs and 18 20-lb. bombs were dropped. 1,800 rds. S.A.A. fired. Returned 05.00 hrs. Two machines, pilots Lt. Reynolds and Lt. Clavey, observers Lt. Hopwood and Lt. Wiseman, left to bomb troops in area Tsaritsin-Gumrak. Good results were obtained. 1 112-lb. and 14 20-lb. bombs dropped. 1,200 rds. S.A.A. fired. Two machines, pilots Lt. White and Lt. Verity, observers Lt. Thompson and Lt. Hopwood, left to bomb Tsaritsin-Gumrak area at 08.30. Good results were obtained with bombs and machine-gun fire. 1 112-lb. and 14 20-lb. bombs dropped. 1,200 rds. S.A.A. fired.

Returned 09.00 hrs. Lt. Clavey and Lt. Hopwood left for reconnaissance of Tsaritsin-Dubovka-Kotlobanski-Karpovka area at 15.00 hrs. Enemy was observed in Gumrak area retreating in N.E. direction. In the morning at 04.00 hrs. enemy was observed evacuating his front-line trenches and all his transport was retreating at full speed along roads and open country towards Gumrak and Elshanka. In evening Volunteer Army occupied the line Elshanka-Grutenka. Machines flew back to Gniloaksaiskaya at 16.30 hrs. Capt. Davis and Lt. White encountered violent thunderstorm and hurricane of wind, but landed safely. Lt. White's propeller was stripped of fabric, and paint was washed off wings by rain.

It will be seen that on the 29th the enemy was observed to have vacated his front-line trenches and to be retreating in the Gumrak area. Gumrak is situated north of Tsaritsin on the railway that runs north-west from that town. Tsaritsin was being evacuated, and by the end of the month the town was occupied by the volunteer army. It was a great triumph for Denikin's forces. There is another point of interest in the above extracts. Davis and White encountered a violent thunderstorm and White's machine suffered badly.

The Caucasian Army under Wrangel pushed forward, and on July the 6th "C" Flight moved up to Beketovka, bombing Kamichin and Sistrenka.

Meantime work at headquarters at Ekaterinodar had been going well forward to equip a further train for "B" Flight. But there were enormous difficulties, as stores and spare parts were missing, and often, even when they did get into the country, were pilfered. As "C" Flight had to be kept up to full strength the work at Ekaterinodar was still further delayed. However, on the 15th of July, the train was ready and sent to Kharkov. On the 19th, however, orders were despatched to Kharkov recalling the train. It was now required for the Volga front, to relieve "C" Flight. Consequently, the new "C" Flight left Ekaterinodar on the 21st of July with Captain Frogley in command. Captain Davis and his flight, who had done such good work, returned from Beketovka. The new "C" Flight carried out its first bomb-raid on July the 23rd, and thence to the end of the month continually bombed Kamichin and Tcherni-Yar.

This flight on July the 30th was responsible for a very gallant piece of work. Three machines, piloted by Captains Frogley, Anderson, and Elliot, with Lieutenants Greenslade, Mitchell and Laidlaw, as observers, carried out a bomb-raid on Tcherni-Yar. The machines came under heavy machine-gun fire from the ground. Captain Anderson and Lieutenant Mitchell were attempting to take photographs of the bombing, and Captain Elliott and Lieutenant Laidlaw were acting as escort. Captain Anderson's machine was shot through the starboard main tank and he turned for home when he suddenly saw Captain Elliot's machine going down, obviously in difficulties. He therefore followed Elliot down, and landed about a quarter of a mile away.

Meantime Elliot set fire to his machine and Laidlaw used his machine gun against the Bolshevik cavalry who were approaching towards the British machines. Elliot and Laidlaw were, however, picked up by Anderson. Lieutenant Mitchell came home—a distance of 110 miles—standing on the lower plane, with his thumb blocking the hole in the petrol tank. The machine got off the field just as the Red Cavalry arrived. Captain Elliot and his observer were thus saved from the hands of the very troops on whom the attack was made. They had been shot down at 1,500 feet by fire from the ground, but, although Captain Anderson's aeroplane was also crippled, he went down to Elliot's help without hesitation. The raid was not abortive. Five 112-lb. and fourteen 20-lb. bombs were dropped on barges and many rounds fired against the cavalry.

During the month of August "C" Flight continued to do good work bombing and scouting over the area of fighting. They assisted in the attack on Tcherni-Yar and in addition bombed Startiskoe, Bilklei, and Dubovka. During the course of these raids an enemy balloon on the Volga was set on fire and totally destroyed and a Nieuport machine standing in front of a hangar was hit and set on fire. The fire spread to the hangar, which burnt fiercely. There was probably a petrol store within.

The squadron suffered two casualties during the month. On the 15th Captain R. E. Eversden was accidentally shot dead by a sentry. On the 28th, whilst bombing the enemy captive balloon at Bilklei, Captain J. L. McLennan was hit by a machine-gun bullet and died before landing.

Here is Baron Wrangel's Caucasian Army Order No. 290, dealing with this episode.

18(31) Aug., 1919.

Tsaritsin.

On the 15 (28) inst. during the aerial scouting and bomb-dropping on the Bykovo, the British officers Captain Anderson, pilot, and Captain McLennan, observer of the 47th Squadron, Royal Air Force, notwithstanding the difficulty of observation in consequence of strong enemy fire, performed their task with the utmost disregard for their own safety, and giving valuable information concerning the enemy and destroying an enemy captive balloon, in attacking which they were forced to descend into fierce rifle fire.

During the performance of this attack, observer Captain McLennan was killed.

For this deed of valour and self-denial, I confer on Captain Anderson the St. George's Cross 3rd Class No. 871,002 and on Captain McLennan the St. George's Cross 4th Class No. 871,003.

(Reference:—Para. 67 and 80 of the St. George Statute.)

(Originally signed)   Baron Wrangel,
Lt.-Gen., G.O.C. Army.

There is a curt but interesting entry in the August *War Diary*. It reads:—

August 5. Today was an official holiday to celebrate the peace.

No work done at Squadron Headquarters.

Whilst headquarters were celebrating the peace, "C" Flight were doing one of the hardest days destruction they had ever done. They were co-operating with the attack on Tcherni-Yar. In the early morning they raided this town. They came back and loaded up again and repeated their raid in the afternoon, and after they had dropped their bombs came down low and fired into the Bolshevik trenches. They returned, and again set out at 5.20 p.m. for a third raid on Tcherni-Yar. Only three machines were available for this work and the total for peace-day was 67 bombs, 2,300 rounds of ammunition, and 16 hours of flying time. A fine achievement, and the officers responsible for it deserve every credit. They were Captains Frogley, Anderson, Elliot, and Palmer, and Lieutenants Cronin, Hatchett, Mercer, Simmons, Greenslade, Mitchell, Addison, and Sergeant Smith.

Some of the best work of the squadron was done during September. On the 14th Major Collishaw, who had been superintending the work at Ekaterinodar and Novorossisk, went to the Volga front. During this month some D.H.9 a's which had arrived were made serviceable, and at the same time "Camels" were received for "B" Flight. Whilst flying one of these "Camels" on the 30th of the month, Captain Kinkead, who was escorting D.H.9's on bombing and photographic reconnaissance, was attacked by an enemy Nieuport, which he proceeded to shoot down into the River Volga. The main work done by "C" Flight during the month was bombing and shooting up enemy troops, transport and dumps. A barge in the Volga which had eight seaplanes aboard received a direct hit and several of the seaplanes were completely smashed. This happened on September the 17th. The work of 47 was the subject of many notes of congratulation from the Russian staff. On the 19th of September the general officer commanding Russian aviation sent a message as follows:

These last few days I have had the pleasure of reading in the daily report of flying of 47 Squadron R.A.F., about the extraordinary work of the British pilots, and especially about Major Collishaw. I beg you to accept and transmit to Major Collishaw from the whole Russian aviation our sincere admiration of his brilliant activity.

The Volunteer Army was sweeping forward, and early in October Headquarters and "A" Flight evacuated Ekaterinodar and joined "C" and "B" Flights at Beketovka. From here raids were continued throughout the month against the Bolshevik fleet and dumps. "B" Flight with their Camels did some effective ground-strafing and the Bolsheviks were severely handled. On the 22nd Major-General Sir H. C. Holman, in command of the British Military Mission in South Russia, and Brig.-General A. C. Maund, commanding the Royal Air Force, visited the flights at Beketovka, and during the week both these officers made several flights over the lines on bomb-raids, etc. Their visit was greatly appreciated by all ranks.

One of the features of the campaign at Tsaritsin — was the success of "B" Flight under Flight Lieutenant S. M. Kinkead, with Camel single-seaters: this flight operated with great success in direct contact with front-line troops and in attacking formations along and behind the enemy front. Perhaps the most significant work done by the flight was the co-operation with General Wrangel's cavalry corps, led by the big-hearted Cossack General Ulyai. Flight Lieutenant Kinkead and his companions would descend and bomb and machine-gun the enemy, causing great disorder, amounting sometimes to panic. Then General Ulyai would attack with his cavalry, to complete the confusion.

The best work of this kind was done in October, during the great Bolshevik counter-attack against Tsaritsin. Dumenko, the Bolshevik cavalry leader, had broken through the junction of the Caucasian and Don Armies on the River Don, some 40 miles west of Tsaritsin, and he was approaching that town from the south-west with no troops to oppose him. The country over which he was advancing is bare *steppe*-land that would hardly offer cover to a rabbit. Flight Lieutenant Kinkead with Captain Burns-Thompson and Lieutenants Daly and Aten located Dumenko's cavalry division and swooped down on to them, firing continuously with their machine guns and dropping their bombs. So determined and so successful was the attack that Dumenko's cavalry were scattered over the plains in all directions and control of them was lost. Tsaritsin was saved from the Bolshevik cavalry and Dumenko's division was not seen on the front for some time after this.

The accuracy of the bombing of this flight, said General Maund, was remarkable. The method adopted was to dive until the target could be seen through the Aldis Sight, whereupon the bombs would be released whilst the machine was still on the dive. Troops, transport, and artillery in position were all attacked this way.

The respect for British aeroplanes which "B" Flight had instilled into Dumenko and his men was shared by the Bolshevik fleet in the

Caspian. During the Bolshevik attack against Tsaritsin, the fleet co-operated with the land troops and actually began to shell Tsaritsin itself. In spite of heavy antiaircraft fire from the shore and from the fleet, "A" Flight under Captain Slatter and "C" Flight under Captain Frogley attacked the fleet again and again until it retired in disorder up the Volga. The fleet never became a serious weapon of offence or defence after that. Indeed prisoners taken some time later stated that when the fleet was ordered to attack again in December there were minor mutinies because it was "murder to come within reach of the English aeroplanes."

It may be argued that the effect obtained by aircraft in these operations was due to the demoralisation of the Bolshevik troops. This would not be quite true. The Red troops fought well enough on the ground but had a real terror of the efficiency of aeroplanes. The mentality of the Russian peasant and the conditions of fighting in South Russia were not perhaps unlike the types met with and the mode of warfare conducted in minor affairs on the outskirts of Empire. Colonel Arthur Lynch, who lectured in Paris in 1902 on the Boer War, paid a tribute to the work of the British balloon sections:

> The Boers took a dislike to the balloons. All other instruments of war were at their command ... but the balloons were a symbol of the scientific superiority of the English which seriously disquieted them.

The latest example of the moral value of aircraft against troops who cannot meet aircraft with aircraft has been the campaign against the Mad *Mullah* of Somaliland, where the Royal Air Force acted as a primary striking force. The power of the *Mullah*, which withstood many land expeditions, crumbled at last to a punitive expedition from the air.

To return to our story, Captain Anderson, who, with Lieutenant Mitchell, had done such continuous and good work, was wounded by machine-gun fire on October the 10th. On the 24th Captains B. G. H. Keymer and W. B. Thompson were killed when starting off on a raid. Both these officers had done splendid work with the squadron.

In September, 1919, there was some question of 47 Squadron being withdrawn from the front at Tsaritsin and being attached to the Instructional Mission in South Russia. This suggestion drew forth a strong letter from Brigadier-General Maund, who had given his constant support and encouragement to the squadron. He gave it as his opinion that the suppression of the squadron would be serious from the moral and political point of view:

"The value of this squadron, the damage it has done to the Bolsheviks, and the moral effect it has had on the Volunteer Army, are so great, that to withdraw it will have a most deplorable effect. They are worth as much as the whole Russian Air Force put together."

He went on to point out that all the officers and men were willing to stay on as a unit of the Russian Volunteer Army, and, if 47 were going to be disbanded, they would prefer to do this. They did not wish to volunteer for the Instructional Mission, as they "had gone to Russia to fight." In the result the unit in South Russia ceased to be known as 47 Squadron in October, 1919, and its extraordinary adventures afterwards can find no place in the doings of that squadron. But a year after war had ceased on the western front, and after four years of active service, the members of the squadron could still protest that they "had gone to Russia to fight"; and to fight they remained. On that note we must take our leave of them.

Appendix 1: Summary of the History of No. 47 Squadron in Macedonia

(A) *Date and Place of Formation.*

Formed in May, 1916, at Beverley.

(B) *Date proceeded Overseas, and Destination.*

Left England on September 5, 1916, for Salonika.

(C) *Subsequent Stations, with Dates of Transfers from one to another.*

No, 47 Squadron arrived at Salonika on September 20th, 1916'

"A" Flight moved from Salonika to Janes on October 20th, 1916.

"B" Flight moved from Salonika to Janes on October 27th, 1916.

"C" Flight moved from Salonika to Janes on October 27th, 1916.

"C" Flight moved from Salonika to Kukus on October 27th, 1916.

"C" Flight moved from Kukus to Snevce on December 4th, 1916.

"C" Flight moved from Snevce to Janes on January 20th, 1917.

"B" Flight moved from Janes to Snevce on January 20th, 1917.

"C" Flight moved from Janes to Kirec on March 2st, 1917.

"A" Flight moved from Janes to Hadzi Junas on May 12th, 1917.

"B" Flight moved from Snevce to Janes on May 13th, 1917.

"A" Flight moved from Hadzi Junas to Kalabac on July 30th, 1917.

"A" Flight moved from Kalabac to Hadzi Junas on October 23rd, 1917.

"A" Flight moved from Hadzi Junas to Kirec on April 7th, 1918.

"A" Flight was transferred to No. 150 Squadron on April 26th, 1918, remaining at Kirec.

"B" Flight moved from Janes to Hajdarli on May 11th, 1918.

"C" Flight moved from Kirec to Janes on May 11th, 1918.

"A" Flight was formed at Hajdarli on August 21st, 1918, the machines being D.H.9's.

"A" Flight moved from Hajdarli to Salonika on October 20th, 1918.

"B" Flight moved from Hajdarli to Salonika on November 3rd, 1918.

Two A.W.'s formed part of a Composite Flight which left Salonika on October 25th, 1918, for Gumuldzina.

This flight moved from Gumuldzina to Dedeagatch on October 29th, and from Dedeagatch to Salonika on November 23rd, 1918.

"B" Flight moved from Salonika to Amberkoi on February 4th, 1919.

"A" Flight moved from Salonika to Amberkoi on February 14th, 1919.

Headquarters and "C" Flight moved from Janes to Amberkoi on February 16th, 1919.

(D) *Types of Machines used, with Dates of Replacements.*

A.W. 90 h.p. R.A.F. (Royal Aircraft Factory) engine.
Bristol Scout.
B.E.12. November 13th, 1916.
De Havilland Scout (D.H.2). February 17th, 1917.
A.W. 140 h.p. R.A.F. February 19th, 1917.
Vickers Bullet. June 23rd, 1917.
B.E.12a. September 22nd, 1917.
B.E.2e. October 20th, 1917.
S.E.5a. November 30th, 1917.
Bristol Monoplane. February 12th, 1918.
A.W. (160 Beardmore). March 2nd, 1918.
D.H.9. August 2nd, 1918.

(E) *Names of Commanding Officers and Dates.*

Major C. C. Wigram in Command.

Major C. C. Wigram ceased to Command on December 23rd, 1916.

Captain J. W. Gordon (Acting), from 23rd December, 1916, until 31st December, 1916.

Major F. F. Minchin, D.S.O., M.C., from January 1st, 1917, until March 13th, 1918.

Major G. D. Gardner, M.C., from March 13th, 1918, until June 5th, 1918.

Captain B. E. Berrington (Acting) from June 6th, 1918, until July 31st, 1918. (Major Gardner in hospital and later evacuated.)

Major F. A. Bates, M.C. From August 1st, 1918, until January 5th, 1919.

Captain F. W. Hudson (Acting), from January 5th, 1919.

(F) *Wings and Brigades in which Squadron served.*
16th Wing, Middle East.

(G) *Such Information as Number of E.A. destroyed or shot down out of control, Weight of Bombs dropped, etc., etc.*

Enemy aircraft destroyed	9
Enemy aircraft captured	1
Enemy aircraft driven down out of control	8
Weight of bombs dropped	54 tons 2½ cwt
Machines lost over the lines	10
Local reconnaissances carried out	360
Army reconnaissances	135
Photographic reconnaissances	773
Escorts	619
Patrols	2,067
Contact patrols	34
Destructive shoots	339
Registrations	1,156

Appendix 2: Casualties

TABLE A.—CASUALTIES (MACEDONIA)

1917	OFFICERS	
Jan. 5	2nd Lieutenant A. D. Pocock	Prisoner of war.
Jan. 15	Lieutenant S. J. M. White	Killed over lines.
Jan. 15	2nd Lieutenant H. Matthews	Killed over lines.
Feb. 11	Major M. A. Black	Killed over lines.
Feb. 12	2nd Lieutenant S. Stopher	Prisoner of war.
Feb. 26	2nd Lieutenant C. McM. Howes	Wounded during bomb raid on Janes aerodrome.
Mar. 12	2nd Lieutenant D. H. Glosson	Killed over lines.
Apr. 5	2nd Lieutenant W. H. Farrow	Wounded in combat.
May 2	2nd Lieutenant J. Watt	Killed in combat.
May 9	2nd Lieutenant E. E. Wheatley	Wounded in combat.
June 24	Lieutenant A. C. Dent	Wounded by anti-aircraft fire.
July 8	Lieutenant H. C. Brufton	Killed—the machine broke in air after fight.
Aug. 20	Lieutenant F. W. H. Thomas	Wounded in combat. Died of wounds.
Aug. 20	Lieutenant H. A. Jones	Wounded in combat.
Oct. 3	2nd Lieutenant G. C. Gardiner	Wounded in combat.
Oct. 6	Lieutenant E. R. Wilkinson	Wounded in combat. Died of wounds.
Oct. 16	2nd Lieutenant P. C. Hunter	Killed in accident.
	Lieutenant A. S. Butler	Killed in accident.
Oct. 29	2nd Lieutenant P. D. Montague	Killed over lines.
Oct. 29	2nd Lieutenant J. R. Gubbin	Prisoner of war (died of wounds).
Nov. 12	2nd Lieutenant J. Boyd	Injured in accident.
Nov. 14	2nd Lieutenant E. Brewer	Wounded in combat.
Nov. 30	Captain R. M. Wynne Eyton	Wounded in combat.
Nov. 30	2nd Lieutenant W. D. Robertson	Wounded in combat.
Nov. 30	2nd Lieutenant J. C. Nelson	Injured in accident.

133

1918	OFFICERS (contd.)	
Jan. 1	2nd Lieutenant H. A. Tracey .	Prisoner of war.
Jan. 1	Lieutenant A. Rowan . . .	Prisoner of war.
Jan. 17	2nd Lieutenant G. C. Gardiner .	Injured in accident.
Jan. 29	2nd Lieutenant M. M. Wilson .	Killed in accident.
Jan. 29	2nd Lieutenant J. S. Jones . .	Injured in accident.
April 6	2nd Lieutenant R. C. Vaughan .	Wounded by anti-aircraft fire.
April 24	Lieutenant A. V. Morton . . .	Injured in accident.
May 7	Lieutenant C. J. Page . . .	Wounded by anti-aircraft fire.
June 24	Lieutenant D. L. Graham . .	Killed : brought down by anti-aircraft fire.
June 24	2nd Lieutenant A. G. Kane . .	Killed : brought down by anti-aircraft fire.
July 26	Captain C. H. Taylor	Wounded by anti-aircraft fire.
Sept. 18	Lieutenant J. A. Brandt . . .	Killed : brought down by anti-aircraft fire.
Sept. 18	2nd Lieutenant H. Gerhardi . .	Killed : brought down by anti-aircraft fire.
1917	OTHER RANKS	
Feb. 2	17691 Act. Corpl. De Pomeroy .	Killed.
Feb. 2	31384 2 A.M. A. Chalmers . .	Killed.
Feb. 2	14417 2 A.M. W. Parkinson .	Killed.
Feb. 2	18096 2 A.M. W. Chambers . .	Killed.
Feb. 2	41410 2 A.M. G. Clutterbuck .	Killed.
Feb. 2	32758 2 A.M. R. Ward . . .	Killed.
Feb. 2	1170 Pte. McGrath (attached) .	Killed.
Feb. 2	740 Flight Sergeant R. Tansley	Wounded (died Feb. 27, 1917).
Feb. 2	5528 Sergeant W. Swingler . .	Wounded.
Feb. 2	8996 Sergeant W. Hemmings .	Wounded.
Feb. 2	13690 1 A.M. T. Waterhouse .	Wounded.
Feb. 2	15094 1 A.M. W. Davies . . .	Wounded.
Feb. 2	14079 1 A.M. A. J. Underwood .	Wounded.
Feb. 2	21983 1 A.M. A. Dunn . . .	Wounded.
Feb. 2	30641 1 A.M. N. Johnson . .	Wounded.
Feb. 2	26812 1 A.M. H. Kelf . . .	Wounded.
April 7	10096 2 A.M. E. C. Rawson . .	Accidentally killed.
Oct. 29	10018 2 A.M. T. H. Bury, Aerial Machine Gunner	Missing (prisoner of war).
Nov. 28	16849 1 A.M. F. T. Rotsey . .	Wounded in night bomb raid on aerodrome.
Nov. 28	18732 2 A.M. T. Black . . .	
Nov. 28	19208 2 A.M. J. Thorne . . .	
Nov. 28	11259 2 A.M. W. Goodman . .	

1917	OTHER RANKS (contd).	
Dec. 28	51553 Sergeant R. Fisher . .	Injured in face in aeroplane accident.
1918		
June 1	40156 1st Cl. Pte. G. H. W. Archer (Sal. A.P. attd. 47th Squadron)	Accidentally injured.

TABLE B.—CASUALTIES (SOUTH RUSSIA)

1919		
Aug. 15	Captain R. E. Eversden . . .	Accidentally shot by sentry.
Aug. 28	Captain J. L. McLennan . .	Killed by fire from ground.
Sept. 25	Lieutenant A. H. Day . . .	Wounded by anti-aircraft fire.
Oct. 10	Captain Anderson	Wounded by machine-gun fire.
Oct. 24	Captain B. G. H. Keymer . .	Killed in action.
Oct. 24	Captain W. B. Thompson . .	Killed in action.

Appendix 3: Honours and Awards

TABLE A.—HONOURS AND AWARDS (MACEDONIA)

1. *Immediate Awards.*		
1917.		
February 2nd . .	Lieutenant C. ff. Denning	M.C.
March 2nd . . .	Captain W. D. M. Bell .	Bar to M.C.
September 2nd .	Lieutenant F. W. H. Thomas	M.C.
September 2nd . .	Lieutenant H. A. Jones .	M.C.
1918.		
February 8th . .	2nd Lieutenant J. S. Jones	M.C.
April 11th . . .	Sergeant P. Spargo (Pilot)	D.C.M.
October 11th . .	Captain J. R. Milne . .	D.F.C.
October 11th . .	Lieutenant J. C. F. Holland	D.F.C.
2. *New Year's Honours*		
January, 1917 . .	Captain W. D. M. Bell .	M.C.
3. *Birthday Honours.*		
June, 1917 . . .	Lieutenant E. R. Wilkinson	M.C.
	2nd Lieutenant R. E. Buckingham . . .	M.C.
4. *New Year's Honours*		
January, 1918 . .	Major F. F. Minchin, M.C.	D.S.O.
	Captain W. R. B. McBain	M.C.
	Lieutenant H. J. Scales .	M.C.
	Captain R. M. Wynne Eyton	M.C.
5. *Birthday Honours.*		
June, 1918 . . .	Captain J. C. O. Dickson	D.F.C.
	167. Flight Sergeant (T/ S.M.) May, A. R. . .	M.S.M.
6. *New Year's Honours.*		
January, 1919 . .	Lieutenant J. Boyd . .	D.F.C.
	Lieutenant L. J. Collier	D.F.C.

January, 1919	2nd Lieutenant C. P. Primrose	D.F.C.
	Captain H. G. Davis	D.F.C.
	2nd Lieutenant G. H. A. Hart	D.F.C.
	Lieutenant M. MacEwan	D.F.C.
	2468. Sergeant Lovelace, F.	M.S.M.
	3786. Flight Sergeant Ostler, C.	M.S.M.

7. *Mentions in despatches.*

July 21st, 1917 . . Lieutenant J. R. Wilson
740. Flight Sergeant Tansley, R. J. C.

November 28th, 1917 Captain W. D. M. Bell
Lieutenant H. J. Gibson
Captain W. R. B. McBain
Major F. F. Minchin
Lieutenant H. J. Scales
Lieutenant W. Sutherland
Lieutenant R. M. Wynne Eyton
25407. Corporal Young, J. L.

June 11th, 1918 . Lieutenant P. A. A. Boss
2nd Lieutenant J. S. Jones
Captain W. R. B. McBain
Lieutenant F. D. Travers
5650. Sergeant Sprott, R.

January 30th, 1919 Major F. A. Bates
Captain H. G. Davis
Lieutenant R. D. de Pass
2nd Lieutenant G. H. A. Hart
Lieutenant F. A. Whitfield
Lieutenant J. Boyd
Lieutenant L. J. Collier
Captain S. B. Edwards
2nd Lieutenant T. H. Formby
Lieutenant M. MacEwan
2nd Lieutenant C. P. Primrose
19256, Sergeant Hare, W.

January 30th, 1919	20403, Sergeant Parker, I.	
	25459, Corporal Thomson, J.	
	18011, Acting Corporal Wilson, A.	
	2834, Sergeant Dowsett, T.	
	3786, Chief Mechanic Ostler, C.	
	11778, Chief Mechanic Swinburne, W.	

8. Foreign Decorations.

1917.

March 5th . . .	Captain J. W. Gordon .	Croix de Guerre.
March 31st . . .	2nd Lieutenant R. E. Buckingham . . .	Croix de Guerre.
August 22nd . .	Lieutenant F. W. H. Thomas	Croix de Guerre with Palm.
August 22nd . .	Lieutenant H. A. Jones .	Croix de Guerre with Palm.
1918.		
November 7th . .	Captain J. R. Milne . .	Croix de Guerre.
November 7th . .	2nd Lieutenant T. H. Formby	Croix de Guerre.

NOTE.—In addition to the above, some officers who served with No. 47 were decorated after transfer to other units in the 16th Wing. In some cases the decorations were awarded partly because of their good work with 47. For example, Lieutenant G. C. Gardiner, Lieutenant C. B. Spackman, Lieutenant J. A. Beeney, who received the D.F.C. whilst with No. 150 Squadron, and Captain C. Hodgkinson-Smith, who received the M.B.E. and Croix de Guerre whilst with 16th Wing Headquarters.

TABLE B.—HONOURS AND AWARDS (SOUTH RUSSIA)

DISTINGUISHED SERVICE ORDER.

Flight Lieutenant W. F. Anderson.
Observer Officer J. Mitchell.

Flight Lieut. S. G. Frogley.
Flight Lieut. S. M. Kinkead, D.S.C.

BAR TO DISTINGUISHED FLYING CROSS.

Flight Lieutenant W. Elliot, D.F.C.

DISTINGUISHED FLYING CROSS.

Observer Officer R. Addison, M.C.
Lieutenant E. J. Cronin.
Flying Officer A. H. Day.
Flight Lieut. S. G. Frogley.
Flight Lieut. N. Greenslade.

Flying Officer J. R. Hatchett.
Lieutenant H. Mercer, M.C.
Lieutenant H. E. Simmons, M.C.
Flight Lieut. W. Burns Thomson.
Flight Lieutenant F. W. Hudson.

MERITORIOUS SERVICE MEDAL.

204378 S.M.1. J. Hoskins.
313012 F/Sgt. P. Armitage.
80210 Cpl. C. E. Smith.
329917 A.C.2. W. Hardy.
295915 A.C.2. J. A. Cranwell.
60797 A.C.1. T. Humphrey.
238686 F./Sgt. M. F. G. Mill.

66305 Sgt. F. J. Smith.
49891 A.C.1. G. Green.
228135 L.A.C. M. S. Beaver.
241058 A.C.1. S. Boak.
156102 A.C.2. R. Blount.
126785 A.C.2. N. Pamphilon.

ORDER OF ST. ANNE, 2ND CLASS WITH SWORDS.

Major R. Collishaw.

ORDER OF ST. ANNE, 2ND CLASS.

Captain S. M. Kinkead.

Captain W. Burns-Thomson.

ORDER OF ST. ANNE, 3RD CLASS WITH SWORDS.

2nd Lieutenant G. P. Hopwood.
Lieutenant C. P. Primrose.
2nd Lieutenant W. Mann.

Lieutenant E. J. Cronin.
Lieutenant J. R. Hatchett.

ORDER OF ST. ANNE, 3RD CLASS.

Captain H. H. Crickitt.

ORDER OF ST. STANISLAS, 2ND CLASS WITH SWORDS.

Major R. Collishaw.
Captain S. G. Frogley.

Captain W. F. Anderson.
Lieutenant J. Mitchell.

ORDER OF ST. STANISLAS, 3RD CLASS WITH SWORDS.

Lieutenant N. Greenslade.
Lieutenant H. Mercer.
Lieutenant R. Addison.
Lieutenant H. E. Simmons.
Lieutenant A. H. Day.
Lieutenant H. W. A. Buckley.
Lieutenant A. H. Hollis.

Captain W. F. Anderson.
Lieutenant J. P. Armitage.
Captain H. H. Crickitt.
Captain W. Burns-Thomson.
2nd Lieutenant A. M. Verity.
Lieutenant J. M. Webb.

ST. GEORGE'S CROSS, 3RD CLASS.

Captain W. F. Anderson.

ST. GEORGE'S CROSS, 4TH CLASS.

Captain W. Elliot.
Captain S. J. Palmer.
Captain S. G. Frogley.
Captain R. Addison.
Captain H. G. Davis.
Lieutenant E. G. Clavey.
2nd Lieutenant C. C. Reynolds.
Lieutenant J. M. Webb.
2nd Lieutenant W. Mann.
Lieutenant E. S. White.
2nd Lieutenant A. M. Verity.
Lieutenant C. P. Primrose.

2nd Lieutenant G. P. Hopwood.
Lieutenant H. S. Laidlaw.
Lieutenant H. E. Simmons.
Lieutenant H. Mercer.
Lieutenant J. Mitchell.
Lieutenant J. R. Hatchett.
Captain S. M. Kinkead.
Lieutenant B. Thompson.
Captain W. Burns-Thomson.
Lieutenant E. J. Cronin.
Captain W. F. Anderson.

ORDER OF ST. VLADIMIR, 4TH CLASS WITH SWORDS.

Captain W. F. Anderson.
Captain W. Elliot.
Lieutenant H. S. Laidlaw.

Lieutenant J. Mitchell.
Captain S. M. Kinkead.
Captain W. Burns-Thomson.

ST. GEORGE'S MEDAL, 4TH CLASS.

66305 Sgt. F. J. Smith.
313012 Sgt. P. Armitage.
30258 F./Sgt. A. Reeves.
25407 Sgt. J. H. Young.

113368 L.A.C. R. Smith.
34911 A.C.1. J. McCorquodale.
139703 A.C.2. Morris.
60797 A.C.1. T. Humphrey.

SILVER MEDAL ON ST. STANISLAS RIBBON.

204378 Sgt.-Maj. J. Hoskins.
200599. Sgt.-Maj. H. P. Finch.
682 F./Sgt. W. Hannah.
25 F./Sgt. M. Goodchild.
49891 A.C.1. G. Green.
241058 A.C.1. S. Boak.

126785 A.C.2. N. Pamphilon.
329917 A.C.2. W. Hardy.
30258 F./Sgt. A. Reeves.
Cpl. C. E. Smith.
Cpl. Braund.

Macedonia—Final Air Operations, 1918

With the formation of a fighting squadron, No. 150, in April 1918, air superiority passed to the British, and it was retained until the end of hostilities. No. 150 Squadron began with one flight from each of Nos. 17 and 47 Squadrons, actually transferred on the 26th of April: the third Flight was formed independently on the 7th of May. The two original Flights took with them S.E.5a's and Bristol monoplanes, but the third Flight was equipped with Sopwith 'Camels'. (The strength of the squadron at the Armistice was 9 S.E.5a's, 7 Sopwith 'Camels', 1 Bristol monoplane, and 1 B.E.12).

The first of the bombers for which Lieutenant-General Sir G. F. Milne had asked were not received until August 1918, nearly a year after the request had been made. On the 21st of August No. 47 Squadron, which had worked with only two flights of Armstrong-Whitworth's since the transfer of a flight to No. 150 Squadron in April, was brought up to strength with the formation of a flight of D.H.9 aeroplanes. (3 At the armistice No. 47 Squadron had 10 Armstrong-Whitworths and 6 D.H.9's. Major F. A. Bates had succeeded Major G. D. Gardner in command of the squadron on the 1st of August.)

No. 17 Squadron worked with two flights until the 14th of June, when a third flight was formed, but the squadron remained under strength until September, when a flight of D.H.9's arrived as reinforcements. (At the armistice No. 17 Squadron had 9 Armstrong-Whitworths, 6 D.H.9's, and 1 B.E.12.)

During the summer of 1918, therefore, the two corps squadrons were not up to establishment, but the few up-to-date fighters of No. 150 Squadron so dominated the enemy air service that Nos. 17 and 47 Squadrons were enabled to increase their offensive bombing activities, in which they were helped from time to time by naval air detachments stationed at Thasos and Stavros. The two-seaters of Nos. 17 and 47 Squadrons, other than the D.H.9's, could be employed for bombing only if the observers were left behind, and protection was therefore provided by fighting escorts from No. 150 Squadron.

Notable bombing targets were the aerodromes at Hudova, behind the Dojran front, and at Drama on the Struma front. On the morning of the 8th of May, as an example, twenty aeroplanes from Nos. 17 and 47 Squadrons, escorted by fighters from No. 150 Squadron, bombed Drama. Eighteen of the same bombers attacked the aerodrome again in the afternoon, and sixteen naval aircraft also bombed the same target during the day: damage was done to hangars and to aeroplanes on the ground.

On the 13th of May ten aeroplanes from the detachment working at Thasos, under the orders of the Rear-Admiral, Aegean, flew to Marian aerodrome for two days' work in co-operation with Nos. 17 and 47 Squadrons. On the journey to Marian the naval bombers made a diversion to attack an enemy dump at Chepeldze, and after taking on a new load of bombs at Marian they attacked the dump at Marinopolje station, which had been previously bombed by fourteen aeroplanes from Nos. 17, 47, and 150 Squadrons. Next day the main targets were the dumps at Livunovo and Kakara, and the station at Demir Hisar, all squadrons taking part, after which the naval aeroplanes flew back to their base at Thasos.

On the 23rd of May sixteen aeroplanes from Nos. 17 and 47 Squadrons, escorted by eleven fighters from No. 150 Squadron, dropped 1¼ tons of bombs on the aerodrome at Hudova on the Dojran front. Such bombing as that instanced above was in pursuance of Lieutenant-General Milne's wish to strike at the enemy through the only medium open to him. At the end of May, however, there were bombing attacks which aimed at helping Allied military operations west of the Vardar. General Guillaumat, Commander-in-Chief of the Allied Armies of the East, was planning an offensive on the Macedonian front, and by way of rehearsal, and with the further object of testing the quality of the Greek troops under his orders, he decided to capture about eight miles of front trench system, from north-east of Ljumnica to north of the village of Lunzi.

To keep the enemy in doubt about the place of attack, artillery bombardments and raids were variously made by the French, the British, and by the Serbs. The British began with a bombardment on the front of the 22nd Division on the 28th of May, and the fire was extended to the front of the 26th Division next day. On the 29th, when the 7th South Wales Borderers made a raid on the Dojran front, ten aeroplanes, with an escort of eleven fighters, bombed the station, dump, and aerodrome at Hudova. On the same day an aeroplane observed for the fire of the 424th Siege Battery (8-inch howitzers) which had been loaned to the French for direct support on the main front.

At 4.55 a.m. on the 30th of May the Greek infantry began their attack, and not long after they had started ten Royal Air Force aeroplanes again bombed Hudova, the objective being the aerodrome, where hangars were damaged and a petrol dump set on fire: these air attacks were part of the British activity to divert the attention of the enemy. The whole action was brilliantly executed, the enemy was taken by surprise, and the Allied troops captured all their objectives on the 30th of May, together with 1,812 prisoners. The victory, although a minor one, caused elation in Greece, where it helped to consolidate the position of M. Venizelos and to cement the unity of the Greek Army.

From May onwards there were important changes in the dispositions of the British troops as a result of the taking over of a part of the Struma front by Greek divisions. The situation from the sea to the Vardar about the middle of July, when the movements had been completed, was as shown in the sketch, facing. While the moves were being made there were indications that the Bulgarians were preparing an offensive. Early in June air reconnaissance reports showed that Bulgar ammunition dumps behind the Dojran front had increased in size, as had camps and dumps in the Strumica valley. Furthermore, although enemy aerodromes appeared unchanged, there was more activity in the air than for some weeks, and many combats resulted. The signs that the Bulgars might be preparing an attack were confirmed from an unexpected quarter.

Towards the middle of June deserters began to cross to the British lines in unusual numbers, and they brought with them the same story—that they had surrendered to avoid taking part in a battle which was about to take place between Lakes Dojran and Tahinos. Lieutenant-General Sir C. J. Briggs, commanding the 16th Corps, with the approval of Lieutenant-General Milne, took full precautionary measures, but on the 17th of June newly arrived deserters gave the information that the attack, which had apparently been planned to coincide with the Austrian offensive on the Piave on the 15th of June, had had to be cancelled on account of a mutiny among the Bulgar soldiers. As soon as it was clear that there would be no enemy attack relief movements on the British front were resumed.

Meanwhile, the French general, Guillaumat, had been suddenly recalled to an appointment in France, and he was succeeded as Allied Commander-in-Chief by General Franchet d'Espérey, who formally took over on the 18th of June. Both generals were representative of the military genius of their country. Quiet, courteous, incisive, cautious in preparation, but swift and bold in action, each in his turn inspired confidence in the Allied armies on the Salonika front, and each contributed a share to the shaping of the final plan by which the enemy armies in Macedonia were subjugated.

A change of command of the Royal Air Force is also to be noted. On the 19th of June Lieutenant-Colonel G. E. Todd succeeded Lieutenant-Colonel G. W. P. Dawes in command of the Sixteenth Wing.

During July and August there were no important operations on the ground, but the air squadrons did not cease from their bombing attacks, usually made by twenty or more aeroplanes at a time, on aerodromes, railheads, and dumps. In August the work of co-operation with the artillery gradually increased in volume, and the squadrons were also called upon to extend their photography of enemy territory. The reason for this expansion of the work of co-operation was the impending Allied offensive, destined to be the beginning of the end of hostilities. The authorities in England had, from the inception of the Salonika campaign, set their faces against a major offensive in the Balkans, and the strength of the British Army in Macedonia had consequently never exceeded what was necessary to maintain a defensive role. How the Salonika front came to be the scene of the first decisive campaign of the war makes curious and interesting reading, for which the student is referred to the official military history of the campaign. (*Military Operations, Macedonia*, by Captain Cyril Falls.) Although everything was ready, it was not certain until the 10th of September that the Allied Governments would agree to the offensive. On that day, however. General Franchet d'Espérey received a telegram sent by Monsieur Clemenceau in Paris to inform him that full agreement had at last been reached and that he was authorized to begin the Salonika operations when judged desirable.

General Milne, when expressing to the British War Office his adherence to the plans for the Allied offensive, had stated that success on the front allotted to the British army was unlikely if he did not receive necessary reinforcements. His demands were modest. He asked only for sufficient additional personnel to bring his units up to strength, and for a small reinforcement of artillery. He would, however, require a considerable increase of ammunition, in particular of chemical

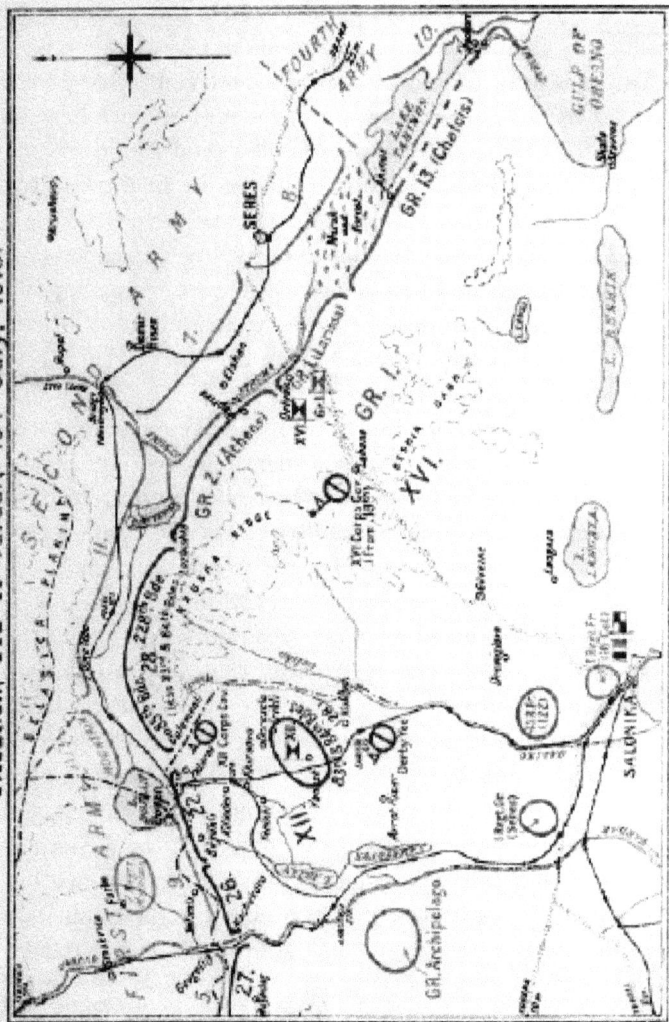

Situation, Sea to Vardar, 15th July, 1918.

shell. He was weak in heavy artillery for counter-battery work and it was his opinion that this weakness could best be mitigated through the employment of gas shell by which the enemy batteries, many of them sunk in elaborate concrete emplacements, might be neutralized. Finally, he stood in urgent need of spare parts for his mechanical transport, and of motor tyres and inner tubes. In the result the British commander-in-chief received only a modicum of what he asked for. What happened was that the British authorities 'at home gave their approval to the attack but did not supply the means which he declared to be necessary.' (*Military Operations, Macedonia*, vol. 2.)

The task of the British Salonika Army in the final offensive, difficult enough, was made more difficult by the failure to send the reinforcements and equipment judged by the British commander-in-chief to be essential. The anxieties of General Milne are sympathetically set out in the official military history and it would be out of place here to make further reference to the subject. What is of particular interest, however, is that those anxieties derived in some measure from the activities of German bombing squadrons on the Western Front. On the night of the 11th of August 1918 German bombers destroyed No. 2 Base Mechanical Transport Depot at Calais, and the spare parts, tyres, and inner tubes for a majority of the British transport vehicles in service on the Western Front became ashes. The situation which resulted called for exceptional remedial measures, and indeed the disaster was on a scale which precluded any early possibility of attention to the wants, no matter how serious or urgent, of outside theatres of war.

How far the German bombers were also responsible for the shortage of shells on the Macedonian front cannot be exactly determined. Between the 19th and 22nd of May 1918, however, the bombers had destroyed more than 12,000 tons of ammunition as a result of successful attacks on two British main ordnance depots on the Western Front. This did not lead to a real shortage of ammunition in France, but the German success brought home to the authorities the undue vulnerability of the ammunition depots, and, until steps taken to reduce this vulnerability should become effective, anxiety about the supply of ammunition to the Western Front could not be allayed. The least that may be said is that General Milne's request would have received timely and more favourable consideration if the enforced pre-occupation of the home authorities with the ammunition needs of the armies in France had not existed. That air activity in northern France should have some effect upon military plans in Macedonia affords a striking example of the far-reaching results obtainable from successful bombing operations, *provided the targets are well chosen.*

In the offensive plan adopted by General Franchet d'Espérey the main role was allotted to the Serbian Armies. The reader may the more easily appreciate the essence of the plan if he refers to the sketch, facing. The key point was Gradsko, situated at the junction of the Crna with the Vardar, and some thirty-five miles from the front line. If Gradsko could be rapidly taken the chief lines of the Bulgarian communications would be cut or threatened, the enemy forces would be divided, and the way would be opened for a decisive exploitation of the break-through. To advance against Gradsko along the narrow and difficult Vardar valley would be to attack the enemy where he was strongest, and where the chances of success, certainly of an early success, were remote. General Franchet d'Espérey therefore decided to attack from the mountains of the Moglena between the Crna and the Vardar, a formidable starting-point.

On the chosen sector the Bulgars were holding forward positions which appeared to be impregnable, but if these could be carried by surprise in one rush the Serbian troops, fighting-fit and elated, would subsequently be hard to stop, more particularly if the enemy reserves could be pinned down on the remainder of the front.

The first of the secondary attacks which were to follow the main assault was to be made under the orders of General Milne against the Bulgar entrenched system on the high ground between Lake Dojran and the Vardar. The group of divisions immediately west of the Vardar was to link the main Serbian attack with that at Dojran. The opposing forces along the whole front were approximately equal in strength, with the exception that the Allied armies had great superiority in aircraft, a total of about 200 aeroplanes against 80.

A preliminary operation on the British front, to make the enemy believe that a thrust up the Vardar valley was contemplated, took place on the 1st of September. The objective was a forward Bulgar position west of the river known as the Roche Noire salient, and the attack, which was reported by air contact patrol observers and proved entirely successful, was made by two battalions of the 27th Division at 5.30 p.m. At the moment when the infantry were launched four aeroplanes each dropped eight 20-lb. bombs on a regimental headquarters in the village of Gevgeli, and each pilot subsequently fired a few hundred rounds of machine-gun ammunition at ground targets.

One of the aeroplanes (pilot. Captain J. B. Walmsley; observer.

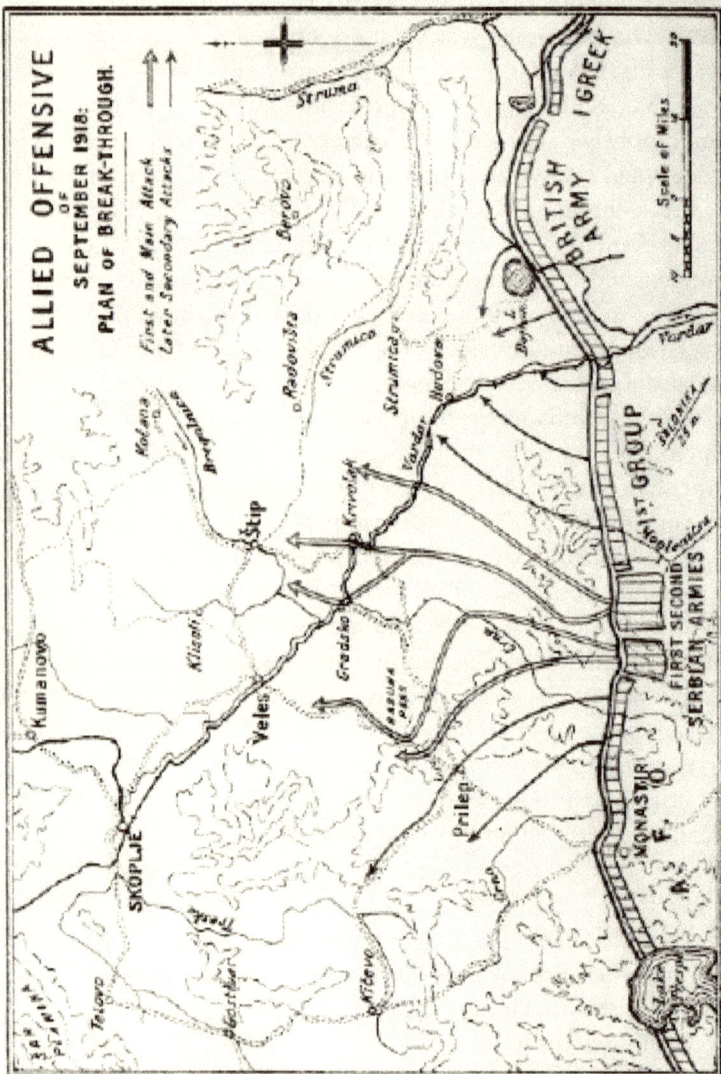

ALLIED OFFENSIVE
OF
SEPTEMBER 1918:
PLAN OF BREAK-THROUGH.

First and Main Attack
Later Secondary Attacks

Scale of Miles

Ordnance Survey 1935

Lieutenant R. D. de Pass) was struck by a bullet which exploded a box of Very lights alongside the pilot and set his coat alight. Under the impression that the aeroplane had caught fire the pilot spun earthwards, but his observer seized the extinguisher and put out the flames. The pilot thereupon came out of the spin and turned for home at a height of 500 feet, but he had not gone far when a tracer bullet hit the engine, which took fire. The observer played on the flames with the extinguisher while the aeroplane was piloted to the nearby aerodrome at Gorgop, where French mechanics finally overcame the fire with sand.

The British military and air activity brought out patrols of German fighting aircraft, but the combats which ensued were indecisive. For a day or two the enemy pilots continued to show themselves rather more than they had done for some time past. On the 3rd of September a formation of six fighters attacked a Royal Air Force photographic aeroplane and its Bristol monoplane escort near Lake Dojran. The monoplane was shot down into the lake, and the last that was seen of its pilot, Lieutenant J. P. Cavers, was when he was struggling in the water clear of his aeroplane under fire from the German aircraft: the reconnaissance aeroplane escaped. The final stages of the combat were witnessed by the pilots of four S.E.5a's as they were making their way home from escorting bombers during an attack on Miletkovo. The S.E.5a's, which were joined by two Sopwith 'Camels', dived on the Germans from 13,000 feet, and a general fight took place about 500 feet from the ground with the result that four of the enemy aeroplanes were destroyed. One British pilot pursued his quarry many miles behind the Bulgar lines and his final burst of fire, which caused the German aeroplane to crash, was aimed from a few dozen feet above the ground.

In preparation for the opening of the great offensive the work of the co-operating squadrons was mainly to help the artillery to register targets, and also photography of the enemy positions. The arrival of D.H.9 aeroplanes made extended reconnaissances possible, and it may be assumed that the passage of Royal Air Force aircraft a hundred miles or so from the front, over places where they had never before been seen, impressed the enemy people in a way which made them readier to throw their hand in after the Allied offensive had broken the defence lines. The D.H.9's set out on journeys which totalled as much as 300 miles, and photographs were taken of such distant centres as Kyustendil and Radomir. It is of interest that the latter town, no more than twenty miles south-west of Sofia, proclaimed a republic before the month had ended, and sent its menfolk, 6,000 or so strong, marching upon the capital.

The artillery bombardment, of great intensity, which preceded the Franco-Serbian assault on the main front, began at 8 a.m. on the 14th of September, and through the long day the mountains echoed and re-echoed with a thunder they had never known. At 5.30 a.m. on the 15th the assaulting divisions, French and Serbian, making up the Serbian Second Army, jumped from their trenches to begin the advance. Behind them were the supporting Serbian divisions, and on their left were the troops of the Serbian First Army, waiting for the right moment to intervene. Lean, skilful, steel-hard, fired and fortified by the conviction that they were about to free their country from the invader, the assaulting Serbs stormed the steep hillsides and won the whole of the Bulgar first line. The French were held for a time, but early on the 16th they, too, had completed their gains, and the front of attack was thereupon enlarged as planned. The advance made on the 16th took the troops forward an additional five miles, through the enemy second line of trenches, and by the end of the following day the attackers had progressed twenty miles from their starting-off places: the way to victory had been opened.

The attack on the British front began on the 18th of September. West of Lake Dojran were the British 26th and 22nd Divisions, the Greek Seres Division, and a French regiment, making up the 12th Corps under Lieutenant-General Sir H. F. M. Wilson. East of the lake was the Crete Division and the British 28th Division under the 16th Corps commander, Lieutenant-General Sir C. F. Briggs. The order of battle of the Royal Air Force units on the morning of the 18th of September was as follows:

Sixteenth Wing Head-quarters	Salonika
(Lieutenant-Colonel G. E. Todd)	
Advanced Head-quarters	Yanesh
No. 17 Squadron (Major S. G. Hodges)	
Head-quarters and 'C' Flight	Lahana
(Armstrong-Whitworths)	
'A' and 'B' Flights	Amberkoj
(Armstrong-Whitworths and D.H.9's)	
No. 47 Squadron (Major F. A. Bates)	
Head-quarters and 'C' Flight	Yanesh
(Armstrong-Whitworths)	
'A' and 'B' Flights	Hajdarli
(Armstrong-Whitworths and D.H.9's)	
No. 150 Squadron (Major W. R. B. McBain)	
Head-quarters and 'B' and 'C' Flights	Kirech
(S.E.5a's and Sopwith 'Camels')	

'A' Flight . . . . Marian
(S.E.5a's)
No. 22 Balloon Company (Captain J. Y. McLean)
26 Balloon Section . . . . Gulemenli
27 „ „ . . . . . . Yeniköi
Aircraft Park (Major C. H. A. Hirtzel) . . . . Salonika

The orders were that 'C' Flight of No. 47 Squadron would be responsible for artillery work, while 'B' Flight undertook contact patrol and close reconnaissance duties, all for the 12th Corps; 'C' Flight of No. 17 Squadron was to work similarly for the 16th Corps, using the former aerodrome of No. 47 Squadron at Snevche as required. Protection for these co-operating aeroplanes was to be provided by fighters from No. 150 Squadron. 'A' and 'B' Flights of No. 17 Squadron were to be ready to answer calls from either of the two British corps for bombing and machine-gun attacks within four miles of the front, and 'A' Flight of No. 47 Squadron was to be responsible for strategical reconnaissance, and for bombing beyond the four-mile limit. No. 26 Balloon Section was at the disposal of the 16th Corps, and No. 27 Section at that of the 12th Corps.

Meanwhile special preliminary air operations had begun on the 14th of September coincident with the opening of the bombardment on the main Franco-Serbian front of attack. On this day five aeroplanes bombed Hudova aerodrome, next day six attacked the station at Demir Kapija, and on the 16th five bombers again attacked Hudova aerodrome and dump. These attacks were on a small scale, but as their object was to help rivet the attention of the Bulgarians to the Dojran front there would have been little point in risking more aeroplanes than judged strictly essential, especially in view of the arduous work which lay ahead once the battle began. On the 17th, the eve of the battle on the British front, what little activity there was in the air was mostly confined to flights in cooperation with batteries engaged on registration.

The infantry attack on the Vardar-Dojran front was launched at 5.8 a.m. on the 18th of September. A distinguished French general who inspected the battlefield after hostilities had ended described it as the 'most terrible' position to assault which he had ever seen, and the author of this history, who knew the greater part of the Macedonian front as it appeared from the air, can testify that the Vardar-Dojran sector stood out as the most intricately formidable part of the Bulgarian line. Had the spirit of the Bulgar troops defending the front been weakened by news of the happenings west of the Vardar the assault would have had chances of success. Those troops, however, if they had knowledge of the real extent of the Franco-Serbian victory, which is doubtful, were unaffected. Their confidence, discipline, and skill were revealed as unimpaired.

Nevertheless, the Greeks, who fought well, captured the foremost position and the intermediate position from Dojran Hill to Hill 340, while the 22nd Division took the enemy front work, known as 0.6, on the 19th when the attack was renewed. No further ground was won. Although the attacks had failed of their immediate aim, which was to 'gain possession of the "P" ridge and the 'neighbouring high ground, and to exploit this success by all available means', they had achieved the object of pinning down the strong enemy concentration between the Vardar and Lake Dojran, and they had compelled the Bulgars to engage their local reserves. It has sometimes been said that an attack on a smaller scale would have had the same result, but, in the words of the military historian:

> The Bulgarians, with their excellent observation posts, were in a position to distinguish at once between a demonstration and a genuine attack. (Falls *Macedonia*, vol. 2.)

During the two days' fighting the aeroplanes did what was necessary in the way of reporting upon the movements of the attacking infantry and of the enemy, but the nature of the struggle was such that their chief usefulness was to indicate the positions of the active enemy batteries. Altogether 151 wireless calls for fire upon hostile guns were sent down from the air on the 18th, and 121 on the 19th, and many of the calls received adequate response. Owing to the smoke and the dust of the barrage fire the air observers could obtain their information, whether of the progress of the battle or about active hostile guns, only by flying near the ground, often below the line of the observation posts on the Grand Couronne and 'P' ridge. All the aeroplanes were hit by shell splinters or by bullets, but the wonder is that no more than one fell on the battlefield: it was directly hit by a shell and crashed in flames.

On both days there were bombing and low flying attacks with machine-gun fire in the immediate battle area, notably about the Grand Couronné, and bombing attacks on dumps behind the front. One D.H.9, fitted with wireless equipment which gave a range of about 100 miles, widely reconnoitred the Bulgar lines of communication in search of concentrations of troops or transport which might form suitable bombing targets: French bombers, using the British aerodrome at Yanesh, were ready to help those of the Royal Air Force as required. During the two days of the battle no exceptional bombing targets were reported, and the bombing attacks were therefore made on the dumps at Cerniste, Cestovo, Miletkovo, and Cinarli.

Little was seen of hostile aeroplanes during the battle. On the morning of the 18th a patrol of four fighters protecting the British contact patrol aeroplanes engaged five enemy single-seaters, which had others in support. Two of the hostile aeroplanes were sent down, and the remainder withdrew. This was the last encounter of its kind on the British Macedonian front: the enemy pilots henceforth left the air to the British.

There was an adventure of an unusual kind on the 19th. Two volunteers were called for to land two British infantry agents behind the enemy lines. The pilots chosen were Lieutenants James Boyd (No. 47 Squadron) and W. J. Buchanan (No. 17 Squadron). The passengers were Lieutenant R. Lamb, Royal Scots Fusiliers, and an unnamed sergeant, and their task was to obtain information about enemy movements in certain areas. Flying a B.E.2e, Lieutenant Boyd landed at dusk near the River Stara about five miles north of Strumica, apparently unseen. In less than a minute his passenger. Lieutenant Lamb, had set out on his mission, and the aeroplane had taken off again. The second aeroplane, which was last seen by the escorting pilots to be flying low down in the darkness in some sort of trouble, did not return.

The passengers who were landed carried four pigeons each, by which they were to communicate their information, but they had instructions that if capture appeared certain they were to release the pigeons without messages. One had male pigeons, the other females, and on the 20th two of each sex returned with no messages. When the war had ended Lieutenant Buchanan was released from a prison at Philippopolis, and he related the story of his adventure.

I left Yanesh aerodrome at 17.00 hours on the 19th September, 1918, with a sergeant who was to be landed near Petric, and crossed the enemy lines at 18.00 hours at about 11,000 to 12,000 feet. I circled over the town of Petric several times and eventually selected a suitable spot to land about four miles due north of the town. I planed down and made a good landing in a field, but unfortunately a party of German troops proceeding along the Petric-Strumica road, whom I had not seen, had apparently noticed my approach and taken cover behind trees and hedges. As soon as I touched the ground, they immediately opened fire at about 600 yards to 700 yards range. My passenger at once got out of the machine and ran off towards some bushes, pursued by a party of Germans.

I then got out of the machine myself and started my engine, which had stopped on landing; I also threw out the cage containing pigeons. I managed to take off and climbed to about 3,000 feet when my engine commenced to give trouble. I tried again and again to gain height to enable me to clear the Beles mountains, but I was obliged to descend and landed a second time, between Petric and Marinopolje.

My engine then suddenly "picked up" and I again took off but could only reach 800 feet, at which height I essayed to travel through the Rupel Pass in order to avoid the hills. I had only covered a short distance when my engine completely gave out and I was forced to glide down and crashed in the bed of the river, having had one wheel shot away and two rifle bullets through a cylinder, presumably at my first landing. Bulgarian soldiers rushed towards me shouting "Bulgar or English?" On telling them that I was English they fired at me at point-blank range, but the firing was very wild and the shots went in all directions, leaving me untouched. As they continued to fire, I ran towards the hills, hoping to find cover, but they came after me and I was very soon overtaken as I was hampered by the extra flying clothes I was wearing. I caught hold of the nearest soldier, gripping him by the shoulders, and called upon the others to stop firing. I handed my revolver to this man, but he immediately dropped it, being afraid of it. The others then came up and went through all my pockets, but only cleared my cigarette case. They then conducted me to a Regimental H.Q. at Vetrina. . . .

He goes on to tell how he was put on trial and informed that he would be shot, but how he was eventually treated as an ordinary prisoner of war.

After the two-day Battle of Dojran there was a brief breathing-space. Both sides had suffered heavily, the attackers more than the defenders, and on the 20th the British and Greek troops were engaged in relief movements and re-organisation. Air reconnaissances on the 20th reported no important enemy activity, except that there were trains, with steam up, facing north in the stations at Hudova and Demir Kapija: there was also a train at Hudova alongside the aerodrome.

The operation orders issued to the squadrons on the evening of the 20th allotted the usual artillery and close reconnaissance duties to the co-operation flights for the next day. On the morning of the 21st, however, about 8 a.m., loud explosions were heard from the British lines far into the enemy area, and it was not long before the aeroplane observers were bringing back news which left no doubt that the Bulgars were, at long last, turning their backs upon the Dojran-Vardar defences. The most comprehensive information was given in a reconnaissance report made by the observers in two D.H.9 aeroplanes which left at 8.30 a.m. to inspect the Strumica Valley-Negotino-Hudova area.

The aeroplanes returned at noon and the officers told of widespread movements. The hangars had disappeared from the aerodrome at Hudova, the dumps and buildings were burning at Cestovo, there had been a notable clearance of military stores and camps at Demir Kapija, there were fires blazing in Krivolak and Gradsko, at Rabrovo there was much crowding of mechanical transport vehicles, and there were as many as 500 lorries and wagons waiting their turn to move along the Kosturino defile.

The 12th Corps commander promptly issued orders that all defensive work was to cease, and that the troops were to be given a short rest preliminary to an advance. Every available aeroplane was ordered to bomb the enemy troops and transport. Thirty-two separate flights were made and a total of fourteen 112-lb. and two hundred and twenty-nine 20-lb. bombs were dropped. The main targets were the troops and crowded transport in the Kosturino defile on the Strumica-Rabrovo road, and when the bombs had been dropped the pilots and observers fired all their machine-gun ammunition into the luckless columns. Not many bombs failed to find a mark, so exceptional were the targets, and lorries, men, and animals were blown in all directions.

In the late afternoon two aeroplanes directed artillery fire on bridges near Furka: while these artillery observers were flying about their work, they had a wide view of the destruction of military stores which was in progress in the enemy area, and one of them counted no fewer than sixty-four separate fires.

There was a gale blowing on the morning of the 22nd when the bombing was resumed. Seven 112-lb. bombs and a hundred and two of 20-lb. weight were dropped on enemy columns during the day, mainly in the Kosturino pass. At noon a telegram had been received from General Franchet d'Espérey saying that the enemy was in retreat along the whole front from Monastir to Lake Dojran, and that the retreat must be turned into a rout by an unceasing and resolute pursuit. General Milne's orders issued for the 23rd stated that the advance was to be continued with the greatest possible speed.

On the 22nd, and again on the 23rd, there were long-distance reconnaissances, nine on the 22nd and seven on the following day. The object was to find out as much as possible of the movements of the enemy, and to discover in particular whether the Bulgars were taking up any specific defensive positions. The information brought back by the observers was that there were no signs that the enemy troops intended to make a stand. It is easy to be wise in retrospect and it has been suggested that the D.H.9 aeroplanes, the most valuable bombing aircraft with the squadrons, should have been employed for offensive operations at this time, and that no more than the minimum strength should have been diverted to reconnaissance.

There were, however, many reasons why the British command needed to be reassured about the enemy intentions. There were grave elements of danger if the Bulgars should make a counter-offensive, and no doubt the very full information provided by the air observers enabled the British commander-in-chief to push his troops forward in pursuit of the enemy faster, because with easier mind, than if he had received only scant knowledge of the hostile activities. The army command was in the best position to judge the needs of the situation, and its appreciation was that the aeroplanes were better employed on reconnaissance than on bombing attacks. About 40 light-weight bombs were dropped on the retreating columns on the 23rd, and a few thousand rounds of machine-gun ammunition were fired at troops.

On the 24th air reconnaissance reports showed that the enemy movements continued northwards in full force. On the Struma front, where reconnaissances were made by the single-seaters of No. 150 Squadron, a withdrawal was also reported to be in progress. Five of the Armstrong-Whitworths of No. 47 Squadron found targets of troops and transport in the neighbourhood of Strumica on the morning of the 24th and dropped thirty-six 20-lb. bombs which were seen to inflict casualties and damage. Two Armstrong-Whitworths of No. 17 Squadron attacked transport and troops again in the evening. None of the D.H.9's was in action on the 24th. On this day three aeroplanes from the naval contingent at Mudros arrived at Amberkoj, the aero-

156

drome of No. 17 Squadron, to help in the operations. On the 25th there were fourteen bombing flights, during which a total of twelve 112-lb. and eighty 20-lb. bombs were dropped.

The Germans have stated that the Bulgarian First Army became demoralised as it retreated, and there can be no doubt that the British aeroplanes contributed much to this state of affairs. In the battle fought at Dojran on the 18th and 19th of September the Bulgarian First Army had suffered severe losses, although less severe than the British and the Greeks. The Bulgarian troops had revealed fine soldierly qualities, and it is known that their spirit remained high after the battle. As they proceeded to make their enforced withdrawal, they might draw such comfort as they could from the knowledge that the difficulties of the country made it extremely unlikely that the British and Greek troops would be able to effect a rapid pursuit.

Although the units of the Bulgarian First Army may have become aware, as they went back, of the demoralisation in the ranks of the defeated Bulgarian Eleventh Army, it seems doubtful whether such well-tried soldiers would have collapsed so soon if it had not been for the air bombing offensive to which, as was made painfully clear to them by the disappearance from the air of German pilots, there could be no answer. By the 25th of September the demoralisation was such that, in the words of the official military historian:

The British and Greeks between Lake Dojran and the Vardar were troubled more by the nature of the country than by the resistance of the enemy.

On the 26th the three bombers from Mudros (two D.H.9's and one D.H.4) attacked the aerodrome and railway sidings at Livunovo, and eight other pilots at intervals bombed troops and transport between Strumica and Yenikoi. On this day the Sixteenth Wing headquarters moved with general headquarters from Salonika to Yanesh, and 'C' Flight of No. 17 Squadron moved from Amberkoj to an aerodrome at Stojakovo. Next day there was considerable mist which impeded air work, but four aeroplanes bombed at various times, notably columns in the Kryesna pass on the Struma front. On the 28th air reconnaissances revealed that the Kryesna road was 'choked with transport'. Pilots made two or three journeys and there was a total of twenty-nine bombing flights during which one hundred and ninety-four lightweight and five 112-lb. bombs were dropped: all aeroplanes attacked also with machine-guns.

Probably the greatest effect was obtained by six pilots of No. 47 Squadron when they bombed convoys in the Kryesna pass at 5.30 p.m. They carried forty-four bombs of 20-lb. weight, and half of these exploded directly among the transport, blowing some of it off the road, piling up wagons and causing a general panic. When making their way home from a reconnaissance flight which had taken them as far as Kyustendil, the pilot and observer in a D.H.9 saw twelve guns, oxen-drawn, among the retreating columns north of Kryesna. The pilot dived and machine-gun fire was opened from a height of 500 feet: some of the men and oxen were seen to fall. An American diplomat subsequently stated that he was in his motor-car on the road at the time the aeroplane attack was made and that he saw several of the oxen and drivers killed or wounded: he himself had a narrow escape.

On the 29th the mist was thick again. The first air observer over the Kryesna pass in the morning found that the traffic blockage had been cleared during the night, but that columns of transport and troops were on the move south of the pass. Seven pilots set out to attack these columns, and among the sixty-three bombs dropped were three of 112-lb. weight: many direct hits were made. This was destined to be the last offensive air operation and the martyrdom of the Bulgar troops was at an end. Mist and clouds throughout the remainder of the day prevented a continuance of the bombing, and at 10 p.m. a Convention was signed by General Franchet d'Espérey and by plenipotentiaries of the Bulgarian Government in accordance with which hostilities ceased at noon on the following day, the 30th of September. The activities of the Royal Air Force on the morning of the 30th were confined to reconnaissance flights, one of which was made to Sofia, which was found cloud-obscured.

It was possible near the end, and after hostilities had ceased, to gain a closer impression of the results of the bombing attacks. Staff officers who inspected the routes from Cestovo to Kosturino were awed by what they saw. Their observation was summarized in a telegram sent by advanced general headquarters to the Sixteenth Wing, saying:

> The routes from Cestovo valley to Kosturino show signs of the indescribable confusion that must have existed in the retreat of the Bulgar Army. Guns of all kinds, motorcars, machine-guns, rifles, and every kind of war material abandoned. Dead animals are strewn everywhere, indicating that our R.A.F. must have contributed largely to bringing about this state of things.

The intelligence officer of No. 47 Squadron, who had been sent forward on the 26th of September to make such inspection as was open to him at that time, reported 300 transport wagons destroyed in one area with their horses and oxen lying dead. In a ravine there was 'a vast number of pack animals', and at the hospital at Rabrovo more than 700 human bodies had been collected for burial. Every few yards along the Rabrovo-Kosturino road were dead animals, derelict motorcars, transport of all kinds, and in the *nullahs* near the road transport lay tumbled where it had crashed. First-hand evidence of the effect of the bombing in the Kryesna pass is lacking, but there is no reason to believe that it was less devastating.

Although Bulgaria had laid down her arms, the war was not over. The German supreme command, however, to whom the rapid collapse of Bulgaria had come as a surprise, had no illusions. They knew that the position of Austria-Hungary and of Turkey had been made extremely hazardous. General Franchet d'Espérey decided to direct his full attention to the Danube, rather than to Constantinople, and he ordered a bold forward movement. The British troops began to advance accordingly, but as the result of an interchange of views between General Milne and the authorities at home, and between the British and French Governments, the Allied plans were modified and the task allotted to a newly assembled army under the command of General Milne was to secure the passage of the Dardanelles to enable the Fleet to take action against Constantinople.

Before this decision was arrived at, the opportunity was taken to overhaul the aeroplanes, transport, and stores of the Royal Air Force squadrons. Some of the aeroplanes were employed to convey officials on important missions to Sofia and other places. When it was settled that the British army would move against Turkey, a Royal Air Force officer was sent to make a selection of suitable landing-grounds. Reconnaissances, meanwhile, were made by No. 47 Squadron from the former German aerodrome at Drama. It was decided to send a flight from No. 17 Squadron for co-operation with the 16th Corps from an aerodrome near Philippopolis, and to organise a Composite Flight from Nos. 47 and 150 Squadrons for work with the 12th Corps from an aerodrome near Gumuljina.

An advanced convoy moved out to Philippopolis, on their 250-mile journey along bad roads, on the 19th of October, and two aeroplanes followed a few days later. The Composite Flight followed their transport to the aerodrome near Gumuljina on the 25th. On the 31st of October, before the various movements of the Royal Air Force units had been completed the armistice was signed with Turkey.

A Bombing Stunt, and Afterwards

Blackwood's Magazine 1918-10 Vol 204 Iss 1236
By Ballast

1

After a little warm tea and biscuits in the Mess, we stroll on to the aerodrome, and the machines take off. Ours is the only two-seater, and my job is chiefly as gunner. We anticipate some trouble before we return—and we get it.

The rendezvous is over the aerodrome at 6,000 feet. At this height we form up six machines, and at a signal from our leader head for the lines. I settle down comfortably and take in the glorious panoramas open to our gaze. Many have attempted to describe the beauties of earth as seen from a mile or two above it. It surely is indescribable in its grandeur. The country in this part of Macedonia is wonderful. As I look towards the Beles Dagh, the 7,000-feet range that rises like a wall from the shores of Lake Doiran to the Struma Valley, the morning sun just rising tips the whole of this ridge with a delicate pink.

The lake itself comes shortly into view and reflects in its depths the beauties of the mountains and the early morning sky. We have now climbed a bit and I can distinguish the line of the sea very faintly many miles away. In the same direction Mount Olympus rises big and mighty. It is obvious why Olympus should be chosen as the seat of the gods. I have seen it from near and far and all directions, and, although only some 9,000 feet high, it always looks ethereal and its summits seem to soar high above the reach of mortals. What would the gods think could they look out on this troubled land now—or do they still *"sit beside their nectar, careless of mankind?"*

We pass high over a "Sausage," and I think more of business and less of the panorama. We are now passing over the trenches. There is very little shelling. Some of our heavies are tickling the Bulgar up a bit on the Pip ridge, a wonderfully fortified position. A Hun field battery is firing at our trenches near the Jumeaux Ravine. I spot his flashes and mark down his position for a little return hate when I get back. I never pass over the Jumeaux Ravine without thinking of that ghastly night when it ran red with English and Bulgar blood. Many a man who roamed as a boy the quiet lanes of the West Country and spoke its soft accent has found a grave in those Serbian hills just below.

"*Wouf, wouf, wouf!*" Archie raps out furiously. The Bulgar hates our bomb raids, and has collected a formidable group of Archies on this part of the front; and he makes very good shooting with them.

"*Wouf!*"—a deafening and the old bus shakes violently as I put my head into the office. Tommy—my pilot—turns to laugh. That was a near shave, but our only injury is a tear in one of the lower planes. Archie gets unpleasant when you have bombs aboard. Suddenly Archie ceases. I look quickly round, and there, coming at us from out the sun, are four Huns. Three of our machines, which are scouts and form the escort, spot them too and turn to meet them. Our leader goes straight ahead and we follow, leaving our escort, who are much faster, to drive off the Huns and catch us up.

Aerial fighting is always difficult to follow, and as we drew farther away, I could not distinguish what was happening. Plenty of lead was being pumped from the guns, and the Hun tracer-bullets, with their thick trail of smoke, were much in evidence. I looked around and saw a large formation of machines like flies in the distance, and scented them as Huns. We could only hope they did not spot us.

Meanwhile we are passing over an aerodrome, and machines are taking off in all directions, climbing rapidly towards us. Our objective is still miles away. There is no sign of our escort returning, and our position begins to look a bit sticky. Every mile seems endless, and we drag along like an exhausted motor-lorry. At long-last I sight our objective—a very important H.Q. At the same time two of our escort appear—the other has had to return owing to engine failure. The first machine drops its bombs and turns for home, The second is slightly in advance of us and a bit higher. I look up as it gets over the objective, and see its last big "pill" start on its journey.

It is curious to watch a bomb rush past you. It looks so harmless—like a piece of scrap-iron falling off a roof. A second or two later a great spurt of red smoke and debris goes up into the air as the bomb finds its mark, and a few more names are added to the enemy casualty lists. We turn to unload our pills, and I spot a Hun scout about 800 feet under our tail. I long to have a pot at him, but cannot afford to squander ammunition. Our bombs dropped, we start for home, and as we do so I see a squadron of six fast Hun scouts—our old friends the flies on the horizon—diving towards us. The only machine behind us is one of our own scouts. The other scout, having finished his ammunition in a scrap on his own with two Huns, is now with the other two bombers slightly ahead of us.

I swing my gun on to the foremost of the Huns, waiting for him to come within effective range. At the same time our scout has spotted the machine that I mentioned was climbing on our tail, and dives on him. As he does so the six Huns dive on him. He must have been killed almost instantly, for he started to spin and went crashing to the earth below—one of the best of pilots and men. I fire on the Huns, and must have hit the leader in a vital spot, for he falls steeply and goes crashing down out of control. The remaining five turn sharply on to our bus, and attack ere I have time to change my drum. The racket is awful. Eight machine-guns are pumping lead at us from short range. I can hear the bullets hissing past and spitting about the machine, like hailstones.

I opened fire almost as soon as they did, but the first of their bullets got me in the stomach, and doubled me up in the cockpit. I bob up again, feeling a bit muzzy, and carry on firing. I turn quickly to Tommy to get him to swerve a bit to unmask a Hun who has come right up to our tail. But poor old Tommy is sitting back with a face white as death and his eyes closed. I think he has gone West, and so perforce turn to fight it out. The old machine flies straight ahead steadily and evenly, so that I have a steady aim. My left hand is now shot off the gun and begins to spurt blood. It has stopped an explosive bullet. This rather handicaps me in changing drums.

In the next burst I am lucky enough to smite another Hun in a nasty spot, for he goes down out of control, and, as was confirmed afterwards, crashes. In the fighting which follows, yet another Hun goes down in a vertical nose-dive; whether he has been badly hit or merely had enough, I do not know, but anyway he is one the less. Another bullet explodes with a crash on my machine-gun, and sends its pieces into my chin, which bleeds profusely. I hesitate to put my hand up for fear my chin should come away. The remaining Hun machines are now doing better shooting, and my gun is put out of action with three bullets, one of which smashes the gas cylinder. I turn again to Tommy, but he is still oblivious of his surroundings.

163

I am feeling a bit dazed by this time. My hand and face are still bleeding. What happened within the next minute or two I do not quite remember. Either Tommy fell on to the joy-stick or else he went down intentionally. Anyway, the next clear vision I have is of some Hun horse lines not a hundred feet below. A Bulgar or Hun soldier nearby gets a colossal wind up at sight of us diving on him, and hares down the side of the field in great style. Forgetting that my gun has gone I turn it on to him. Then I realise how hopeless our position is.

There seems nothing for it but to bump placidly down among the horses. I picture our announcement in the casualty lists as wounded and missing, I already see ourselves convalescing at Sofia, and hope the Bulgars will let us go about the city on parole. These confused thoughts rush through my mind as I turn to Tommy, who is dazedly conscious now. I ask him if he is going to land, and I look around for a more or less clear spot. Suddenly, however, the engine takes on a less doleful sound; it has been spluttering and coughing up to this, and the hope which springs eternal surges through our beings again.

Then I witness a wonderful struggle of British grit and courage. With a bullet through his back, paralysed down the left side and barely conscious through loss of blood, Tommy controls that machine through a murderous fire from the ground. In a series of zigzags we struggle towards the lines, nearly fifteen miles away. To my joy I recognised the ruins of M——r in the distance. This town is just behind our lines. On we go. Then with a prayer of thanksgiving on my lips and wild joy in my heart we pass slowly over the enemy trenches. Nothing seems to matter now. Despite the guns that are trained on to us we go steadily on.

As we cross No Man's Land and pass our own trenches I give vent to my joy in a blood-soaked cheer, at which Tommy smiles broadly. I think he is going to land in the first available field, but he keeps dead ahead and eventually makes a perfect landing on our aerodrome twelve miles farther away.

I scramble out of the machine and fall into the welcome arms of two Italian tommies, one of whom supplies me with a badly squashed cigarette from the depths of his breeches pocket. Tommy is lifted out and we are laid side by side smoking contentedly.

2

A kindly French M.O. arrived on the scene and gave us a rough dressing. He looked glum at sight of Tommy's wound, and I heard afterwards that they did not expect him to live. Meanwhile the other machines had landed, most of them badly shot about. After what seemed hours, an ambulance arrived and took us on to the French C.C.S. at Florina. Never shall I forget the journey over those broken Serbian roads. The heat was now intense, and the flies began to swarm. The pain that Tommy had to bear on his broken back with each jolt of the car, which went at a snail's pace, was awful. A French surgeon met us half-way with morphia—blessed morphia!—and thence the journey was better. We passed little groups of men on the march—Serbs and Italians and columns of transport. Now and again, we caught arresting glimpses of wooded mountains and fields of dying poppies.

At Florina we received immediate attention, and got between clean sheets. During the week we had in this clearing station we received many visits and messages of congratulation from our friends, General Sarrail and the French Minister of Health came to see us. The officer commanding the French Flying Corps paid us constant visits and was very kind to us. These visits did much to help us forget pain. But how we longed for a white-capped nurse! Alas! our orderlies were Annamites from far-off China, and my French often failed miserably when I asked them to get me anything.

And then that night orderly! I wish I could say he stuck to his post all night. I am afraid he did not. I suspect strongly that he went back to bed after reporting at night. I could never get hold of him. The day orderly I managed to offend in some way. I asked him to get me some water. He chose to construe my French idea of this sentence into an accusation of theft, and he became threatening and hostile. My explanations made matters worse, and for the rest of our acquaintance I went in fear of him. I used to drop into troubled slumber only to dream that innumerable Huns were diving on me, and as they came nearer, they were transformed into grinning faces of Annamites with their cruel slits of eyes. Oh, those nights of clammy heat!

In a bed near mine was a French captain with two bullets in his stomach. I was told he was past hope. He was in a terrible condition, and had been lying there for nearly two months, as he could not be moved. He was riding to a camp when he was attacked by some brigands or comitadjis, whose object was the theft of his horse. Some of them were caught, and a punishment such as they could appreciate was meted out to them. The cheerful patience with which that captain bore his tortures awaiting the end was wonderful. Someone had presented him with a bottle of champagne. Apparently, he was forbidden or unable to drink this, and insisted that Tommy and I should drink his health in it.

That afternoon B. and L. came in to see us, and we split the champagne with them. However, my palate was stronger than my stomach. That evening, I developed malaria, and Tommy followed suit. The fever dogged our paths for the next two months, and when I think of the: heat and the flies and the mosquitoes, my memories of Macedonia are not too pleasant. The morning after we went into hospital the gentle Hun did two bomb raids on Florina. One bomb dropped very near the hospital, and it was with mingled feelings that I saw a great spurt of debris go into the air as I looked through the window. A sudden rattle of machine-guns announced the fact that our people were up, and a little later we heard the great news that three of the Hun machines—all two seaters—had been shot down in our lines, and that three or four of the wounded survivors were on their way to the hospital.

Meanwhile some victims of the raid—all civilians except one Greek soldier—were brought to the hospital. An old Greek woman, who was swathed in black, had evidently lost someone dear to her. She emitted a most creepy sort of wail and rushed to and fro under my window most of the day, refusing to be comforted, When the Huns arrived, two of them were placed one on either side of the French captain. The others went to another part of the building. Of these two, the elder, an *oberleutnant*, died the next night. The younger one, who was about nineteen, and who told me he had not been flying long, was burnt about the head and knocked about a bit from his crash, He had been shot down by B. When B. came along to see us, he brought an explosive bullet which had been taken from this fellow's machine-gun.

Armed with this, I told our Hun friend that I had been wounded by an explosive bullet. He denied that they used them, and when I produced this one from his machine, he became uneasy and explained that his mechanic must have put them there without his knowledge. He was obviously frightened, and I played on his fear by telling him that he was liable to be shot for being found with ammunition forbidden by all laws of civilisation. This bit of information made quite an impression on him. He was moved to the base next day, and although I assured him before he went that he would be well treated, he was still scared, and I am sure heartily repentant of ever having seen an explosive bullet.

I shall never forget the night before we left. We were both pretty bad, thoroughly exhausted by the flies and the damp heat. The Macedonian fly in midsummer is at his worst, The whole room was black with them, and they start to buzz around at dawn. They specially choose sick victims. Their *modus operandi* is to settle in swarms on every sensitive part of your body. Your job is then to pick them off. It is useless to wave your arms about—nothing short of actually pulling them off with your hands is good enough.

When septic wounds are being dressed, Mr Fly, who likes to share a find, brings up whole battalions of his pals from the kitchens. These batten on you as an aperitif before being served up with your beefsteak later. We got a certain amount of relief from mosquito nets, but these were terribly stuffy to sleep under in the daytime. Somehow a few stray flies get under the net and torture you so to let them out that you suddenly fling off the net in disgust and give yourself over to the whole of them.

Very early the next morning we bade farewell to our hospital friends at Florina. The ambulance journey to the railhead, a distance of some miles, was fraught with pain. This road winds along at the foot of a minor wooded mountain at whose foot also Florina is charmingly situated. As we passed through its cobbled streets, native women dressed in wondrous colours glanced casually into the ambulance. The town itself is a quaint mixture of European and Turkish, an occasional mud hut shouldering up against a passable imitation of a London suburban villa.

Arrived at the station round about 6 a.m., we were told we could not make Salonika that day, but must journey to another French hospital at a place called Exisoo, only twenty odd miles away. This journey we made on the bottom of a cattle truck, together with some wounded Senegalese. The Serbian driver had a penchant fer shunting. He gathered speed down a slope and then suddenly put on all brakes, thereby causing us to play a form of draughts, the stretchers trying to jump one another in all directions. This did not agree with Tommy's fractured back, and the end of the journey found him on his last legs. It was midday before we got off that train at Exisoo.

Some more of our Chinese friends were acting as orderlies, This hospital was a delightful place, for the marquees were arranged in an ingenious way that stopped any flies from getting in. They also gave us some iced drinks, and we felt we had struck oil. Our stay here was, however, short. The surgeon informed me that an operation at once was imperative, and that Tommy could not think of making the journey to Salonika. He further stated that their operating tents had been burnt down the previous day, and we should have to move on somewhere else immediately. He then bethought him of an English hospital with the Serbian army some distance away, and telephoned them to send an ambulance to fetch us.

This arrived about 8 p.m. with an R.A.M.C. officer, Captain R., aboard. How happy we were to see him and hear plain English once more! We were moved off again (poor old Tommy). It was very cold now at night, and as we occasionally bent round the road, we had glimpses of the clear cold stars reflected in a still cold lake. To hear the orderlies speaking English when we arrived was a tonic. And then a white-capped sister to tend us through the night. We who had hardly seen an English woman for a whole year! And now here was one who was going to nurse us back to health. It seemed too wonderful.

I dropped into peaceful sleep that night with the sister's voice running like cooling water through my fevered brain, and for the t time failed to have nightmares about brother Hun, I was awakened soon after dawn for my journey to the operating theatre, and Tommy followed me for extraction of the bullet from his back. The next six weeks spent in this hospital were awful. Nothing but the untiring and loving attention we received made them possible. For me it was a series of visits to the operating theatre; a nightmare of hot sweltering days and endless nights; torture by flies and fever and pain. Tommy, too, had repeated attacks of fever and some bad kidney trouble.

Yet, looking back on those weeks, one or two things stir me to a smile. The Serbians and English who died in the hospital were buried every morning nearby. An English bugler sounded the *Last Post*, as it seemed, at the very door of our marquee. When we were feeling our feeblest, each morning the mournful notes of the *Last Post* rang out. Occasionally we must both have wondered whether we should hear it on the morrow. . . .

Then there were the golfers. Every evening, as soon as the heat died down, doctors and nurses went out to the links that they had made around the lake. We had a glimpse of the course when we left the hospital. I can't imagine any scenery more glorious than that enclosing this course—this bit of England hedged round with wild mountains.

Our journey to Salonika was uneventful but long. We left our golfers at about 6 am, and, travelling in a cattle truck fitted with twelve stretchers, we arrived at Salonika at 8 p.m. Fortunately I was on a top stretcher, and could catch good views of the country we passed through. The weather was glorious—it was autumn now—and for the first fifty miles the blending of wooded ravines and dark mountains outlined against the blue sky, formed a picture I shall always treasure. Towards Vertekop the scenery is at its best, as the railway passes across a series of rugged ravines which were filled with trees fast crimsoning, and with multi coloured flowers—a wonderful mixture of autumn and spring, of death and hope.

At Salonika we went to No. 28 General Hospital. How many thousands of our Salonika Forces know this place opposite Dadula! In our blue-covered beds we were carried out each day, and just lazed in the sun until he began to set behind Mount Olympus on the other side of the bay. How we enjoyed those days! And then there were three other fellows from our squadron in the same ward, W——, an observer, with a hole through his leg, caused by an explosive bullet. He had been in the hospital six months, and was a sort of mascot, G——, a pilot, with a bullet in the leg, He had been at Mons with the cavalry, and wandered on to various other fronts without ever having leave. He was cured before we left the hospital, and went back to fly again. And D——, who had a piece of Archie in the leg. D——, who looked as mild as a Hun professor, had the courage of a lion and an excellent repertoire of after-dinner stories.

Then there were two bonnie Scots from the A. and S. They had been wounded in a raid. One of them had fallen into the enemy trench and sat up to find a Bulgarian officer levelling a rifle at him. He promptly replied with his revolver. His shot killed the Bulgar, and the Bulgar's shot wounded him rather badly. He used to rehearse this feat in his sleep nightly, inviting the "boys" in a loud voice to "come on and give it 'em hot."

We had many visitors to see us, including an officer who had commanded Tommy's company in German S.W. Africa. Altogether we were very sorry when the time came for us to move on to Malta.

We were both on deck to say goodbye to Macedonia, while the hospital ship steamed out of the harbour. Tommy was now hobbling a little on crutches, and was looking much better. As we left the sun was dropping behind Olympus in a blaze of colour only seen in the Mediterranean in autumn. The charred minarets of the city, tinged almost to crimson by the sun's last rays, stretched like mighty blood-stained arms to heaven. Everywhere gaped the ruins of the disastrous fire, which destroyed most of this ancient city of many vicissitudes. As we got farther away, we lost sight of the details of the place, and saw it, as I shall always recall it, lying like a pearl in the lap of its encircling blue hills.

A few delightful weeks at Malta followed. Here again we struck an excellent hospital at Tigné.

Then, at long-last, we left for Blighty in the s.s, *Ghurka*. The *Ghurka* had been mined on its previous trip, and all the wounded—mostly amputation cases—had been transferred to tugs and destroyers, in a very heavy sea, without incurring a single casualty. She had not sunk, however, and had back to Malta, where she was patched up and took us aboard. Her engines gave in soon after we got out of harbour. We managed to crawl back into port, where she was put right again, and the following day we said goodbye to Malta for the second time. We had an excellent journey home, although, on one very dirty night, we picked up an S.O.S. from a City liner that had been torpedoed.

We arrived at Bristol early on a Sunday morning in a snow blizzard. England looked very drab and cheerless after the colour and warmth of the Mediterranean. Yet what did any of us care, for we had sunshine in our hearts.

Unfortunately, in London, Tommy and I went to different hospitals, and three weeks later, just as I was recovering from an operation, I got the news that Tommy had died of his wounds,

He was buried at Brookwood Cemetery. Far away from his native Rhodesia, but in a corner of that England for which he gave his life, he lies. God rest his soul!

www.ingramcontent.com/pod-product-compliance
Lightning Source LLC
Chambersburg PA
CBHW021107090426
42738CB00006B/538